EDLP versus Hi·Lo Pricing Strategies in Retailing

Schriften zu
Marketing und Handel

Herausgegeben von Martin Fassnacht

Band 15

Sabine El Husseini

EDLP versus Hi·Lo Pricing Strategies in Retailing

Literature Review and Empirical Examinations in the German Retail Market

Bibliographic Information published by the Deutsche Nationalbibliothek
The Deutsche Nationalbibliothek lists this publication
in the Deutsche Nationalbibliografie; detailed bibliographic
data is available in the internet at http://dnb.d-nb.de.

Zugl.: Vallendar, Wiss. Hochsch. für Unternehmensführung, Diss., 2013

Library of Congress Cataloging-in-Publication Data

El Husseini, Sabine, 1983-
  EDLP versus hi-lo pricing strategies in retailing : literature review and empirical
examinations in the German retail market / Sabine El Husseini.
    pages cm -- (Schriften zu Marketing und Handel, ISSN 1862-605X ; Band
15)
  ISBN 978-3-631-64357-0
  1. Retail trade--Germany. 2. Pricing--Germany. I. Title.
  HF5429.6.G4E52 2014
  658.8'16--dc23
                        2014006555

                          D 992
                      ISSN 1862-605X
             ISBN 978-3-631-64357-0 (Print)
           E-ISBN 978-3-653-03450-9 (E-Book)
             DOI 10.3726/ 978-3-653-03450-9
                   © Peter Lang GmbH
          Internationaler Verlag der Wissenschaften
                 Frankfurt am Main 2014
                   All rights reserved.
    PL Academic Research is an Imprint of Peter Lang GmbH.

    Peter Lang - Frankfurt am Main · Bern · Bruxelles · New York ·
             Oxford · Warszawa · Wien

    This book is part of an editor's series of PL Academic Research
          and was peer reviewed prior to publication.

                      www.peterlang.com

To my parents.

Geleitwort des Herausgebers

Price is the most effective profit driver among the components of the profit-equation "profit = (price x volume) - costs". Furthermore, among the classical 4Ps of the marketing mix, price is the only variable that directly generates revenues, while the other three elements involve expenditures or investments. Especially in retailing, the price is the most important marketing instrument and retail pricing strategy is seen as one of the five most important priorities in retail management. According to most definitions, there exist two main pricing strategies in retailing: The "Every Day Low Price" (EDLP) strategy whereby the retailers claim to offer the lowest every day prices to their customers and the "High-Low" (Hi-Lo) pricing strategy whereby the retailers set their prices on a higher every day level, but use price discounts and promotions to attract customers. In reality, retailers not only use either a Hi-Lo or an EDLP pricing strategy, but follow a "hybrid" pricing strategy containing elements of both Hi-Lo and EDLP.

The work of Dr. El Husseini contains three single parts, in which she answers three research topics. In the first part, she sheds light on the components, determinants and outcomes of pricing strategies in retailing and provides a state of the art literature review about pricing strategy in retailing. In the second part, she uses these conceptual findings and empirically examines the relation between pricing strategy and relevant retail specific outcomes, considering the moderating effects of market/consumer, retail, competitor and brand factors. Dr. El Husseini provides for the first time a detailed measurement of the focal construct "pricing strategy alignment" at the store level. In the third part she investigated the relation between price promotion activity at the category level and the sales dollars per square meter. The results of this study are of high interest for retail managers as they allow them to decide category by category, which pricing strategy is best in order to maximize revenues. Despite the importance of pricing strategy especially in retailing, the topic has been given little attention in the academic research. Dr. El Husseini made great contributions to this research field. In her empirical investigations, she collected a unique, large-scale dataset of objective weekly scanner data containing 34 product categories from 931 retail stores. Furthermore she conducted a qualitative pre-study containing interviews with high-ranked retail managers and CEOs. The selected study area of food retailing has been selected very adequately in the context of the topic. The results show, that retailers are better off in terms of revenue per square meter to choose a pure pricing strategy such as a clear Hi-Lo or a clear EDLP strategy, instead of following a hybrid pricing strategy and getting stuck in the middle.

To sum it up, Dr. El Husseini chose a highly relevant topic both from a scientific and a practical point of view. Her dissertation contains interesting implications for Marketing science and Marketing practice in retailing. I am convinced that this dissertation will encounter in science and practice with great interest.

Prof. Dr. Martin Fassnacht
Holder of the Otto Beisheim Endowed Chair of Marketing and Commerce
WHU – Otto Beisheim School of Management

Preface

The present work was accepted as a dissertation in May 2013 by the doctoral committee of the WHU – Otto Beisheim School of Management. I would like to thank some people who have supported me in the successful completion of the doctoral thesis.

First, I want to thank my first advisor and thesis supervisor Prof. Dr. Martin Fassnacht for his professional support. He was always the person I could trust, the one whom I could discuss both academic and personal issues with and receive great sympathy from.

I would like to thank my second supervisor Prof. Dr. Ove Jensen for providing his timely second opinion. Furthermore, I would like to thank Jun.-Prof. Dr. Tim Brexendorff, Prof. Dr. Walter Herzog, and Prof. Dr. Tillmann Wagner, who supported me with fruitful discussions throughout my thesis preparation process. In addition, I also want to thank Prof. Wayne D. Hoyer and Prof. Jade DeKinder, who were always by my side as dear mentors during my research stay at the McCombs School of Business, The University of Texas at Austin.

This work benefited greatly from the cooperation with partner companies. Therefore, I would like to thank very much all the partners who have supported me with the qualitative and quantitative data collection.

Big thanks also to my colleagues at the chair and at the WHU. Because of them, I will always cherish good memories from my doctoral studies: Katrin Dötsch, Dr. Andreas Ettinger, Hülya Gemril, Daniela Götz, Jan Josten, Philipp Kluge, Jerome Königsfeld, Eva Köttschau, Stephanie Krause, Dr. Jochen Mahadevan, Dr. Henning Mohr, Dr. Yorck Nelius, Dr. Tobias Posner, Dr. Katia Rumpf and Stefanie Wriedt. I would also like to thank Dr. Claas Greger, René Kemmerling, Dr. Julia Lerchenmüller, and Elmar Wyzsomirski for the great time together in Vallendar - I 'm glad to have friends like you.

In particular, I would like to thank Matthias Markmiller for his patience and support during this not always easy time. Without him, I could not have finished this dissertation.

Finally, I would like to sincerely thank my parents, Gabriele and Assem El Husseini. They have always supported me in all stages of my life and were there for me at all times. Therefore, I dedicate this work to them.

Dr. Sabine El Husseini

Table of contents

List of Abbreviations

AIC	Akaike's Information Criterion
ANOVA	Analysis of Variance
BIC	Bayesian Information Criterion
BP	Buying Power
C	Customer's perspective
CEO	Chief Executive Officer
cf.	Confer (compare)
Comp	Competitive Intensity
Disc	Discounter (vs. Non-Discounter)
Dr.	Doktor
Dr. rer. pol.	Doctor rerum politicarum
EDFP+	Every Day Fair Price Plus
EDLP	Every Day Low Price
EDLPP	Every Day Low Purchase Price
Eds	Editors
e.g.	Exempli gratia (for example)
etc.	Et cetera (and so on)
G	Gramm
GfK	Gesellschaft für Konsumforschung
Hi-Lo	High-Low (Pricing Strategy)
HLM	Hierarchical Linear Modeling
HLP	High-Low Pricing
i.e.	Id est (for example)
JBR	Journal of Business Research
JM	Journal of Marketing
JPBM	Journal of Product and Brand Management
JR	Journal of Retailing
JRCS	Journal of Retailing and Consumer Services

M	Mean
MANOVA	Multivariate Analysis of Variance
MS	Marketing Science
p.	Page
PD	Population Density
PPA	Price Promotion Activity
Prof.	Professor
PROMO	Promotional Pricing Strategy
PSA	Pricing Strategy Alignment
QME	Quantitative Marketing and Economics
R	Retailer's perspective
SD	Standard Deviation
SDSQM	Sales Dollars per Squaremeter
SEM	Structural Equations Modeling
SKU	Stock Keeping Unit
SVSQM	Sales Volume per Squaremeter
sqm	Squaremeter
U.S.	United States
WHU	Wissenschaftliche Hochschule für Unternehmensführung
ZfB	Zeitschrift für Betriebswirtschaft

List of Symbols

€	Euro
H	Hypothesis
N	Number of observations
R^2	Coefficient of determination
P	ρ-value
β_0	Intercept
β_j	Regression coefficient
E	Error term
%	Percent

List of Figures

List of Tables

1 Introduction

1.1 Problem background

The equation "profit = (price x volume) - costs" shows that there are just three profit drivers: price, volume and costs. Among these components, price is the most effective profit driver (cf. Simon/Fassnacht 2009, p. 1-5). An increase in price – holding the volume constant – has a 100% impact on profit, whereas an increase in volume – holding the price constant – just influences the profit to the amount of the additional turnover minus the marginal costs (cf. Simon 2004, p. 1084f.). Furthermore, among the classical 4Ps of the marketing mix (product, price, placement and promotion), price is the only marketing mix variable that directly generates revenues, compared to the other three elements which involve expenditures or investments (cf. Monroe 2003, p. 8, Rao 1984, p. 39, Rao/Kartono 2009, p. 9; Sebastian/Maessen 2003, p. 51). Also in retailing, the price is the most important marketing instrument (cf. Ahlert/Kenning 2007, p. 233). Retail pricing strategy is seen as one of the five most important priorities in retail management (cf. Bell/Lattin 1998; Van Ittersum et a. 2010). Tang, Bell, and Ho (2001) even stated that there is nothing more important in business than the right pricing strategy. Through a pricing strategy, the price-performance level of a store is marked out on a long-term basis and thus the framework for further marketing activities is set (cf. Barth et al. 2007, p. 198). The strategic framework represents the basis for all price-political decisions (Liebmann et al. 2008, p. 544 f.). A retailer's pricing strategy has to be developed carefully and is an important issue in order to maximize profits (cf. Ellickson/Misra 2008, p. 813; Gauri et al. 2010, p. 139). Therefore, a pricing strategy is of special importance for the enduring success of companies.

Among retailers, profitability has become a very important concern. Especially grocery retailers operate on very low margins and have fallen into a price-promotion trap, pressured both by competition and consumers (cf. Bolton et al. 2010, p. 301). Over the past years, price wars emerged and price became an even more focal point of retailers' agendas (cf. Diller 2008, p. 500). In times of intensive competition it is getting even more important to create and consequently follow strategies (cf. Möhlenbruch/von Wichert 2002, p. 53) and for retailers to focus on profitable and successful pricing strategies (cf. Bolton et al. 2010, p. 301).

According to most definitions of pricing strategies in retailing, there exist two main strategies. On the one hand, there is the "Every Day Low Price" (EDLP) strategy whereby the retailers claim to offer the lowest every day prices to their customers. The EDLP pricing strategy came up in the 1990s in retailing practice, led by discounters like Wal-Mart which is considered as pioneer of the EDLP principle (cf. Rudolph/Wagner 2003, p. 188). On the other hand, there is a "High-Low" (Hi-Lo) pricing strategy whereby the retailers set their prices on a higher every day level, but use price discounts and promotions to attract customers. Research, as well as observation of retailer behavior, suggests that the motivation for retailers to use an EDLP strategy is the intention of cutting back on promotions in order to improve inventory management, and reduce labor and advertising costs (Voss/Seiders 2003; Levy/Weitz, p. 418; Montgomery 1997, p. 324; Lal/Rao 1997, p. 60). On the other hand, it is suggested that the motivation for retailers to use a Hi-Lo pricing strategy is to "generate excitement, attract shoppers, clear out time-sensitive merchandise and sell complementary, high-martin items," (Voss and Seiders 2003, p. 37). In reality, retailers not only use either a Hi-Lo or an EDLP pricing strategy, but follow a "hybrid" pricing strategy containing elements of both Hi-Lo and EDLP. For example, in the German retail market, Rewe is seen as a Hi-Lo retailer, but Rewe also has EDLP elements with its private label brands. On the other hand, for example Aldi and the drugstore chain dm are pursuing an EDLP strategy, but also offer some products on promotion.

But how is the status quo of research about the topic of pricing strategy in retailing? How many studies have been published and what are the findings? Can these findings be consolidated to derive fruitful avenues for future research and managerial implications? Furthermore, how do these pricing strategies affect the retailers sales performance at the store-level? Should a retailer rather focus on a strong EDLP or a strong Hi-Lo pricing strategy? Or should they stick to a hybrid pricing strategy with both EDLP and Hi-Lo elements? Are there different pricing strategies for different product categories? These questions are of high importance for retail managers.

Despite the importance of pricing strategy especially in retailing, the topic has been given little attention in the academic research, many of the above named questions are still not answered adequately. There has been a huge amount of research on the topic of pricing tactics and especially price promotions in retailing, but a comprehensive examination of pricing strategies in retailing is still missing. Taken together, a better understanding of pricing strategies in retailing, its components, determinants and outcomes both from a theoretical and an empirical point of view is of high relevance for both managers and academics.

1.2 Research questions and outline

The goal of this dissertation is therefore to fill this gap in academic literature and examine the topic of pricing strategy in retailing, both from a theoretical and an empirical perspective. We want to shed light on the components, determinants and outcomes of pricing strategies in retailing. The empirical investigations in this dissertation are based on a large-scale dataset of objective weekly scanner data of German retailers, obtained from SymphonyIRI. The dataset includes a representative product basket with 34 product categories and a sample of 931 German retail stores, for the years 2009 and 2010.

This dissertation contains three single studies, which are presented in chapters 2 to 4. Each study corresponds to a self-contained article manuscript.

The second chapter of this dissertation is based on and follows Fassnacht and El Husseini, 2012. This article has been accepted for publication at the "Zeitschrift für Betriebswirtschaft (ZfB)". Until now no comprehensive literature review about the existing research about pricing strategy in retailing exists. Therefore, we try to fill this gap and provide a state of the art literature review about pricing strategy in retailing in chapter 2. In particular, it deals with the theoretical examination of pricing strategies in retailing with its components, determinants and outcomes. We develop a comprehensive review of the existing literature on pricing strategies in retailing, as claimed frequently in prior research. Thereby, we provide a detailed overview and characterization of the different definitions of the term pricing strategy in retailing. Furthermore, we first differentiate the literature into conceptual and empirical papers about pricing strategy in retailing. Among the empirical papers, we examine and structure the determinants of pricing strategy in retailing that were addressed in prior research, such as "market and consumer factors", "retailer factors: assortment, category, store, chain factors", "competitor factors" and "manufacturer and brand factors". We also examine the outcomes of pricing strategy in retailing, which were identified in past research, such as "retailer outcomes" and "customer outcomes". Finally, we close with a comprehensive research agenda with limitations of our manuscript and directions for future research as well as fruitful implications for managers. For chapter 2, we therefore formulate the following research question:

What are the existing definitions of pricing strategy in retailing? Which components are included in a retailers pricing strategy? Which determinants and outcomes of pricing strategy in retailing have been examined in previous research? Which directions for future research can be derived? What are implications for retail managers?

The study in chapter 3 is based on an unpublished manuscript of the joint authors of Fassnacht, El Husseini and DeKinder (2012). In this study, we use our conceptual findings from chapter two and empirically examine the relation between pricing strategy and relevant retail specific outcomes. For our empirical investigation, we examined an objective scanner data set containing 931 stores from different German retailers. Thereby, we first provide a detailed measurement of our focal construct "pricing strategy alignment" at the store level. This was postulated frequently in prior research, as well as in our theoretical examination in chapter 2. Then, we examine the influence of the pricing strategy alignment on the store performance in terms of sales dollars per squaremeter and the sales volume per squaremeter. Furthermore, we examine the moderating effect of buying power, population density, store format and competitive intensity on the relation between the pricing strategy alignment and the performance outcomes. Finally, we derive managerial implications as well as directions for future research. The research question for this study can be summarized as followed:

How does pricing strategy in retailing at the store level affect the sales performance of a retailer? Is it better to focus on either a strong Hi-Lo or EDLP strategy, or use a hybrid pricing strategy somewhere in the middle? Which types of moderators influence the relationship between pricing strategy alignment and the stores' sales performance? How do these moderators influence this relationship?

Chapter four is based on an unpublished manuscript of El Husseini and Fassnacht (2012). In this study we look beyond the store-level pricing strategy in retailing and investigate the price promotion activity at the category level which is a highly interesting topic especially for retail managers. This was claimed both in prior research and from our interviewees in our qualitative pre-study that we conducted for our study in chapter 3. More detailed, we investigate the relation between price promotion activity and the sales dollars per squaremeter for each of our 34 categories in the sample. Based on our findings, we derive important implications for the retailing practice and give advice which extent of price promotion activity to follow for which category. For chapter 4, we derive the following research question:

How does the price promotion activity at the category level affect the sales dollars per squaremeter? What are managerial implications for the different categories?

In chapter 5, we provide a comprehensive summary and conclusion of the main findings of our investigations in chapters 2 to 4. Figure 1 displays an overview of the dissertation project.

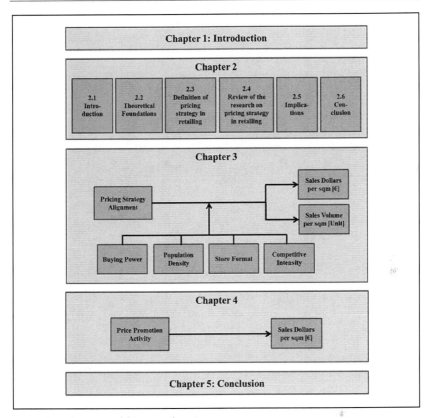

Figure 1:   *Overview of the research project*

2   Pricing Strategy in Retailing – A literature review[1]

2.1 Introduction

The following chapter 2 is based on and follows Fassnacht and El Husseini (2012). As outlined, this chapter contains a comprehensive literature review of the topic of pricing strategy in retailing. It provides the theoretical foundations of pricing strategy in retailing and builds the basis for chapters 3 and 4.

2.1.1 Problem background and relevance of subject

The equation "profit = (price x volume) - costs" shows that there are just three profit drivers: price, volume and costs. Among these components, price is the most effective profit driver (cf. Simon/Fassnacht 2009, p. 1-5). An increase in price – holding the volume constant – has a 100% impact on profit, whereas an increase in volume – holding the price constant – just influences the profit to the amount of the additional turnover minus the marginal costs (cf. Simon 2004, p. 1084f.). Furthermore, among the classical 4Ps of the marketing mix (product, price, placement and promotion), price is the only marketing mix variable that directly generates revenues, compared to the other three elements which involve expenditures or investments (cf. Monroe 2003, p. 8, Rao 1984, p. 39, Rao/Kartono 2009, p. 9; Sebastian/Maessen 2003, p. 51). Also in retailing, the price is the most important marketing instrument (cf. Ahlert/Kenning 2007, p. 233).

Among retailers, profitability has become a very important concern. Especially grocery retailers operate on very low margins and have fallen into a price-promotion trap, pressured both by competition and consumers (cf. Bolton et al. 2010, p. 301). Over the past years, price wars emerged and price became an even more focal point of retailers' agendas (cf. Diller 2008, p. 500). In times of intensive competition it is getting even more important to create and consequently follow strategies (cf. Möhlenbruch/von Wichert 2002, p. 53) and for retailers to focus on profitable and successful pricing strategies (cf. Bolton et al. 2010, p. 301). Furthermore, retailers act under complex circumstances, especially because of broad assortments, and should therefore define a clear framework for their pricing strategy. Until now, in the retailing practice there is

---

1   Based on the manuscript of Fassnacht/El Husseini (2012), accepted for publication in the "ZfB – Zeitschrift für Betriebswirtschaft"

still a tendency towards easy pricing decision rules (cf. Simon/Fassnacht 2009, p. 471-506).

The pricing strategy is seen as one of the five most important priorities in retail management (cf. Bell/Lattin 1998, p. 67). Tang, Bell and Ho (2001, p. 56) even stated that there is nothing more important in business than the right pricing strategy. Through a pricing strategy, the price-performance level of a store is marked out on a long-term basis and thus the framework for further marketing activities is set (cf. Barth et al. 2007, p. 198). The strategic framework represents the basis for all price-political decisions (Liebmann et al. 2008, p. 544 f.). A retailer's pricing strategy has to be developed carefully and is an important issue in order to maximize profits (cf. Ellickson/Misra 2008, p. 813; Gauri et al. 2010, p. 139). Therefore, a pricing strategy is of special importance for the enduring success of companies.

It is traditionally believed, that most retailers use one of two store-wide pricing strategies: the Hi-Lo (High-Low) or the EDLP (Every Day Low Price) strategy. A Hi-Lo strategy involves higher regular prices with steep temporary discounts whereas an EDLP strategy is characterized by consistently low prices (cf. Hoch et al. 1994, p. 16; Gedenk 2002, p. 21-24; Pechtl 2005, p. 292-294; Müller-Hagedorn/Natter 2011, p. 344; Müller-Hagedorn/Preißner 2006, p. 5). Advantages named in the context of Hi-Lo strategy are the increase in profits through price discrimination, the creation of excitement through sales and the possibility for retailers to get rid of merchandise. Advantages of the EDLP strategy are the assurance of customers of low prices, reduced costs and stock outs (cf. Levy/Weitz, p. 418; Montgomery 1997, p. 324; Lal/Rao 1997, p. 60). The EDLP pricing strategy came up in the 1990s in retailing practice, led by discounters like Wal-Mart which is considered as pioneer of the EDLP principle (cf. Rudolph/Wagner 2003, p. 188).

In reality, the retailer pricing strategy is not only a dichotomous variable, but rather a continuum with "hybrid" pricing strategies in between. For example, in the German retail market, Rewe is seen as a Hi-Lo retailer, but Rewe also has EDLP elements with its private label brands. On the other hand, for example Aldi and the drugstore chain dm are pursuing an EDLP strategy, but also offer some products on promotion. A more detailed definition and characterization of the pricing strategies in retailing is given in chapter three.

2.1.2 Goals and structure of the paper

In preparation of this manuscript, we conducted several interviews with high-ranked experts from the consumer goods industry, retailing, consulting, market research and science. Thereby all experts approved that the topic of retailer pricing strategy is highly relevant and different compared to pricing strategies of manufacturers or other firms. Because of the high relevance of the topic of retail pricing strategy, it is necessary to make a comprehensive review of existing research from time to time.

Until now, two papers tried to give a literature review on pricing strategy in retailing. The article of Kopalle et al. (2009) provides a literature review on retailer pricing with a focus on the interaction between pricing strategies and competitive effects. Thereby the authors used the term pricing strategies also for certain pricing tactics. They identified seven competitive factors that determine retailer pricing strategies and derived avenues for future research for each of these effects. Kopalle et al. (2009) focused on two studies (Bolton et al. 2007 and Levy et al. 2004) when building their conceptual framework. The literature base for our article is primarily built on all relevant conceptual and empirical papers on pricing strategy in retailing from leading journals such as Journal of Marketing, Journal of Marketing Research, Journal of Retailing, Marketing Science and many other peer-reviewed journals. Gauri et al. (2010) identified a framework of online and offline retail pricing with determinants and moderators and derived avenues for future research. The authors mostly focused on papers about tactical pricing instruments such as price promotions, pricing decisions, price level etc. rather than on papers about pricing strategy. Our article clearly differentiates from both described papers as we focus on research about pricing strategy and not about tactical pricing instruments in our literature review. Furthermore, our article extends both above named papers in the following ways: (1) we provide a detailed overview of the different definitions of pricing strategy in retailing, (2) we consider the determinants but also the outcomes of pricing strategy in retailing and (3) we provide a comprehensive research agenda for the research field of pricing strategy in retailing.

We found three further conceptual papers from Levy et al. (2004), Grewal/Levy (2007) and Ailawadi et al. (2009) that center the topics of pricing and retailing, but without specifically focusing on pricing strategy. Levy et al. (2004) focused on the determinants of optimal prices rather than pricing strategy in retailing. They identified seven factors that have to be considered to determine optimal prices in retailing (cf. Levy et al. 2004, p. 16). Ailawadi et al. (2009, p. 42) built a conceptual framework with the relationships between manufacturer and retailer decisions on communication and promotion and retailer performance, with focus on the retailer's perspective. The authors examined single retailer decisions among which there are also tactical elements of pricing strategy in retailing. The fact that these two publications focused more on tactical pricing elements rather than on the pricing strategy itself clearly differentiates these studies from our article. Grewal/Levy (2007) reviewed all papers published in the Journal of Retailing between 2002 and 2007 and classified these papers into ten topic categories. Then they highlighted key insights and derived avenues for future research for each area. As the field of pricing strategy in retailing was just shortly mentioned, one cannot speak of a comprehensive literature review. Furthermore, Grewal/Levy (2007) focused on papers from the Journal of Retailing and didn't take into account other peer-reviewed journals as it is done in our paper.

Our manuscript is the first that provides an extensive literature review about pricing strategy in retailing. Based on the theoretical and conceptual foundations (chapter 2), in the third chapter, a comprehensive review of the existing research is given. This is an innovation and development of the existing reviews. For the first time, all relevant articles about retailer pricing strategy are analyzed compactly. In different summary tables (see tables 2-5), the central findings, dependent and independent variables are displayed. In total, six conceptual and 21 empirical papers on pricing strategy in retailing were analyzed. The papers were identified via systematic key word search (pricing, strategy, retailing) in the databases ABI Inform Global, EBSCO/EPNET, JSTOR and Science Direct. Furthermore, the references of the single studies were screened. The paper concludes with a comprehensive future research agenda. We provide fruitful and uncovered avenues for future research which build great potential for researchers in this field. Besides that, managers can use the results to determine how to take into account certain determinants and outcomes of retailer pricing strategy.

2.2   Theoretical foundations of the pricing strategy in retailing

In the following, the theoretical foundations of pricing strategy in retailing are depicted. In some papers the theories that were used were explicitly noted, in other papers not. In the latter case the theories were inferred from the conceptual discussions. Generally and from a strategic point of view, the contingency theory (Ginsberg/Venkatraman 1985; Hambrick 1983a, 1983b; Zeithaml et al. 1988), the market based view (Porter 1991) and the resource dependence theory (Aldrich 1976; Aldrich/Pfeffer 1976; Pfeffer 1972, 1987; Pfeffer/Salancik 1978) are used as theoretical foundations.

The contingency theory, also called contingency approach was developed in the 1960s, stresses the importance of the influence of situational factors on the management of organizations and questions the existence of an optimal way to manage or organize (cf. Zeithaml et al. 1988). One central aspect of this theory is that it is important to specify its determinants to gain an understanding of a business strategy. As a basic proposition, the contingency theory assumes that certain environmental and organizational variables influence strategic orientations systematically. In earlier research, mostly the influence of situative variables like the market dynamic or competitive intensity on the organization structure of firms was examined. In the later research, besides the organization structure, also other organizational variables such as the strategy of the firm were considered (cf. Hambrick 1983a, 1983b; Anderson/Zeithaml 1984; Ginsberg/Venkatraman 1985).

In the center of the methodological procedure of the contingency theory, there are three aspects (cf. Kieser 2006, p. 218):

- Characterization and measurement of organization structures,
- Identification of situative determinants of the organization structure and
- Outcomes of situation-structure-constellations on the efficiency of the organization

We follow this structuring into measurement (overview of definitions), determinants and outcomes when it comes to the literature review on the topic of pricing strategy in retailing in chapter three. Therefore the contingency theory builds an overall framework for our examination.

The market-based approach has its origin in the field of industrial economics (cf. Proff 2002, p. 23). Within this view, the success of a company is explained by the consistent orientation on external circumstances. The market-based view is based on the structure-conduct-performance paradigm from Bain (1956) and Mason (1957) which explains the success of a company through the structure of the industry and the strategic behavior of the company. Michael Porter strongly formed the MBV through his work. According to Porter (1991, p. 97), the success of a firm is determined by the strategic actions of the firm and also by the structure of the branch or industry. Retailers orientate their pricing strategy to the customers, competitors, market and to their own retailer factors such as assortment, category, store and chain. In our literature review in chapter four we will have a closer look at the determinants of pricing strategy in the branch of retailing. Thus, the strong relation between the MBV and our research becomes clear.

The resource dependence theory is characterized through the research of Pfeffer (1972, 1987), Aldrich (1976) Aldrich and Pfeffer (1976) und Pfeffer and Salancik (1978). This theory understands the organization as an open system which is dependent on its environment. The focus of the consideration is the relation between the organization and the actors of the organization environment. The resource dependence theory assumes that organizations are not able to generate all necessary resources by themselves and therefore have to interact with other organizations in order to get the necessary resources (cf. Aldrich/Pfeffer 1976, p. 83). Thereby everything that is necessary for the survival of the organization is considered as a resource: money, physical means, know how, certain behaviors, etc. (cf. Pfeffer 1992, p. 87). The ability of the organization to survive is mostly dependent on the ability, to get access to the necessary resources. The success of an organization is dependent on the ability of the organization to interact actively with the postulations of the interest groups. Regarding the pricing strategy in retailing, customers own important resources for the survival of the company – they own money that they pay to the company for its products or services (cf. Schuppar 2006, p. 47-48).

2.3   Definition of the pricing strategy in retailing

Regarding the existing research on the field of the pricing strategy in retailing it becomes clear that there exists no consistent comprehension of this term. In fact there are many different definitions and interpretations of pricing strategy in retailing. Table 1 shows selected definitions and their focus, before similarities and differences are discussed.

First, most of the definitions include the term "pricing strategy" but there are some authors that use the term "pricing tactic" rather than "pricing strategy" when describing strategies such as Hi-Lo and EDLP (cf. Shankar/Krishnamurthi 1996; Tsiros/Hardesty 2010).

Second, all of the definitions regard the pricing strategy in retailing from the retailer's point of view, not from the customer's point of view. Regarding the strategy literature, this makes sense because it is the retailer's long term decision, and not the customer's decision which pricing strategy to follow.

Third, the majority of the definitions comprise two retailer pricing strategies – Hi-Lo and EDLP – and view pricing strategy as a dichotomous variable (cf. Bailey 2008; Cataluna et al. 2005; Kopalle et al. 2009; Lal/Rao 1997; Lattin/Ortmeyer 1991; Monroe 2003; Neslin et al. 1994; Pechtl 2004). However, many authors point out, that Hi-Lo and EDLP are not just two options of a bipolar classification scheme, but are best seen as the poles of a continuum with hybrid strategies in between (Bell/Lattin 1998; Ellickson/Misra 2008; Gauri et al. 2008; Hoch et al. 1994; Popkowski Leszczyc et al. 2004; Tang et al. 2001). Beyond that, some authors identify even more pricing strategies in retailing. Bolton and Shankar (2003) and Shankar and Bolton (2004) identify five pricing strategies at the store level (Exclusive, Premium, Hi-Lo, Low and

Aggressive Pricing) and at the brand-store level (Exclusive, Moderately Promotional, Hi-Lo, EDLP and Aggressive Pricing). Furthermore, Ortmeyer et al. 1991 suggest an EDFP+ strategy besides Hi-Lo and EDLP.

Fourth, most of the definitions follow a one-dimensional approach concerning the pricing strategy in retailing (cf. Bell/Lattin 1998; Ellickson/Misra 2008; Hoch et al. 1994; Lattin/Ortmeyer 1991; Ortmeyer et al. 1991; Pechtl 2004; Tang et al. 2001). These definitions focus on one single dimension – mostly the dimension of price variation – when measuring pricing strategy in retailing. In contrast, there are authors that have a multi-dimensional approach of pricing strategy in retailing. These multi-dimensional approaches contain promotion and communication decisions in addition to the pricing decisions (cf. Bolton/Shankar 2003; Neslin et al. 1994; Shankar/Bolton 2004; Shankar/Krishnamurthi 1996; Voss/Seiders 2003). Furthermore, some authors also mention service and assortment as additional elements of the pricing strategy and see the pricing strategy more like a positioning strategy (cf. Lal/Rao 1997; Monroe 2003; Ortmeyer et al. 1991). In general, following these multi-dimensional approaches, the pure price focus is not comprehensive enough to mirror the strategic character of pricing strategy in retailing. A pricing strategy should fit in the marketing mix of a firm to serve to reach the firm's goals. Aspects of product-, placement- and promotion strategy should be considered when framing the pricing strategy, if not be declared as a part of the pricing strategy (cf. Lal/Rao 1997, p. 16; Wiltinger 1998, p. 26).

Fifth, according to most of the definitions, the retailer pricing strategy is defined on the store-level, rather than on the assortment-, category- or brand-level. Conventional wisdom sees a pricing strategy as a principle and long-term decision on the store-level (cf. Berekoven 1995, p. 200). Because of its long-term character, the pricing strategy can strictly be separated from the tactical and short-term instrument of price promotions (cf. Scheuch 2007, p. 194-195). Contrary to this point of view, Bolton and Shankar (2003) and Shankar and Bolton (2004) identified the pricing strategies at the brand-store level, not at the store-level. They state, that retailers "customize their pricing strategies at the more fundamental brand-store level, in addition to the store level" (Bolton/Shankar 2003, p. 221).

Table 1:   *Selected definitions of pricing strategy in retailing and their aspects*

Author(s) Year (Page)	Aspects	Definition
Bailey 2008 (p. 211)	• **Hi-Lo/EDLP** *as pricing strategy* • **Store** level • **One-dimensional** approach	• "The pricing strategy can be **every-day low prices (EDLP)** or **promotional pricing – HILO.**"
Bell and Lattin 1998 (p. 67-68)	• **Hi-Lo/EDLP** as **continuum** and *pricing strategy* • **Store** level • **One-dimensional** approach	• "Some retailers position themselves on the basis of 'Low Prices, Everyday' across a wide assortment of product categories, while others offer temporary deep discounts in a smaller group of categories. The former strategy is commonly known as **'EDLP'**, the latter as **'HILO'.**" • "Pure versions of HILO and EDLP seldom exist in practice and **EDLP/HILO is best thought of a continuum**. It is, however, usually possible to differentiate stores according to their relative tendency to operate one format or the other."
Bolton and Shankar 2003 (p. 214-215; 221)	• **Five pricing strategies** (Exclusive/Moderat ely Promotional/Hi-Lo/EDLP/Aggressiv e pricing) • **Brand-store** level • **Multi-dimensional** approach (price/promotion)	• "The distinctive nature of the brand-store pricing strategies underscores the fact that retailers customize their pricing strategies at the more fundamental **brand-store level**, in addition to the store level." • „**Pricing Strategies are multi-dimensional**: prior research has focused exclusively on a single dimension – price variation (i.e. EDLP vs. Hi-Lo pricing) – implying a single pricing continuum. By examining a broader set of measures, our results show that retailer pricing strategies reflect a richer set of dimension - including relative price, deal intensity, and deal support. […] the strategies we have uncovered are combinations of the four independent pricing dimensions, where **each dimension is a separate continuum.**"
Cataluna et al. 2005 (p. 331)	• **Hi-Lo/EDLP** *as pricing strategy* • **Store** level • **One-dimensional** approach	• "[…] two strategies often used in retailing […] are the **every day low prices (EDLP)**, or always low prices, which may be a philosophy applied by discount stores, and the **high and low prices (hi-lo)**, or promotional prices more typical of hypermarkets."
Ellickson and Misra 2007(p. 811; 813)	• **Hi-Lo/EDLP** as **continuum** (with **hybrid** pricing) *and pricing strategy*	• "In many retail industries, pricing strategy can be characterized as a choice between offering relatively stable prices across a wide range of products ([…] **everyday low pricing**) or

Author(s) Year (Page)	Aspects	Definition
	• **Store** level • **One-dimensional** approach	emphasizing deep and frequent discounts on a smaller set of goods ([…] promotional or **PROMO pricing**)." • "This is clearly a simplification […]. Pricing strategies are typically chosen to leverage particular operational advantages and often **have implications for other aspects of the retail mix**. […] In other words, the choice of pricing strategy is more than just how prices are set: it reflects the **pricing dimension alone,** taking other aspects of the retail mix as given." • "[…] The simple EDLP-PROMO dichotomy is too narrow to adequately capture the full range of firm behavior. In practice, **firms can choose a mixture of EDLP and PROMO,** varying either the number of categories they put on sale or changing the frequency of sales across some or all categories of products. Practitioners have a term for these practices - **hybrid pricing**." • "We believe that **pricing strategy is best viewed as a continuum,** with pure EDLP (i.e. constant margins across all categories) on one end and pure PROMO (i.e. frequent sales on all categories) at the other."
Gauri et al. 2008 (p. 256)	• **Hi-Lo/EDLP** as **continuum** (with **hybrid** pricing) • **Store** level • **One-dimensional** approach	• "One of the most powerful and effective strategic tools in retailing is pricing […], for which the options available to retailers range from **everyday low price (EDLP)** to promotional or **high-low (HiLo)** strategies. An EDLP retailer tends to offer lower average prices, whereas a HiLo retailer offers frequent discounts […]. In addition, a few retailers may offer some **combination** (i.e. **hybrid pricing**)."
Hoch et al. 1994 (p. 16-17)	• **Hi-Lo/EDLP** as **continuum and** *pricing strategy* • **Chain-/Store- /Category**-level • **One-dimensional** approach	• "The prototypical description of an **EDLP** pricing policy is: the retailer charges a constant, lower everyday price with no temporary price discounts. These constant everyday prices […] eliminate week-to-week price uncertainty and represent a contrast to the 'Hi-Lo' pricing of […] competitors. The **Hi-Lo retailer** charges higher prices on an everyday basis, but runs frequent promotions where prices temporarily are lowered below the EDLP level."

Author(s) Year (Page)	Aspects	Definition
		• "Although a pure EDLP strategy implies low everyday prices with no temporary price promotion activity, IRI found that 'true' EDLP rarely exists. Instead, it takes on many forms: **chain-wide, store-wide, and category-wide**. Because there are many hybrids, **EDLP is best seen as a continuum**."
Kopalle et al. 2009 (p. 57; 59)	• **Hi-Lo/EDLP** *as pricing strategy* • **Store** level • **One-dimensional** approach	• „Two key retail pricing strategies researched are **everyday low pricing (EDLP)** and **promotional pricing (PROMO)** […]"
Lal and Rao 1997 (p. 60-61)	• **Hi-Lo/EDLP** *as pricing strategy* • **Store** level • **Multi-dimensional** approach (price/promotions, service, communications)	• "**Every Day Low Pricing strategy** is thought to differ from a **Promotional Pricing strategy (PROMO or Hi-Lo)** by not emphasizing price specials on individual goods but instead focusing consumer attention on good value on a regular basis." • "Successful implementation of the EDLP strategy involves communication of relative basket prices, implying that merely setting constant low prices is not viable. […] Our analysis and results offer a **more complete characterization** of the EDLP and PROMO strategies. Indeed, we show that EDLP and PROMO strategies are **positioning strategies**, rather than pricing strategies, **with different elements: price/promotions, service and communications.**"
Lattin and Ortmeyer 1991 (p. 3-5)	• **Hi-Lo/EDLP** *as pricing strategy* • **Store** level • **One-dimensional** approach	• "The strategy (**EDLP**; note from the authors) is typically characterized by retail prices, stabilized on an everyday basis, at a level in between the regular and discount prices of promotional retailers. […] The **promotional retailer** sets a low promotional price and a high regular price."
Monroe 2003 (p. 499-500)	• **Hi-Lo/EDLP** as *aspect of positioning strategy* • **Store** level • **Multi-dimensional** approach (price, advertising, service)	• „The choice of **everyday pricing versus high-low pricing** is an aspect of a firm's positioning strategy. That is, firms that pursue either of these pricing formats must also choose **unique combination of advertising, price and service.** "
Neslin et al. 1994 (p. 1-2)	• **Hi-Lo/EDLP** • **Store** level • **Multi-dimensional**	• "There are three characteristics of retail pricing that appear important in comparing **EDLP and Hi/Lo**: (1) the **frequency of in-**

Author(s) Year (Page)	Aspects	Definition
	approach (price)	**store price cuts**, (2) the **depth of such price cuts**, and (3) the **duration of the price cuts**. [...] EDLP pricing should involve less variation in prices, i.e. price cuts that are not as steep, not as frequent, and longer in duration."
Ortmeyer et al. 1991 (p. 3; 5; 55-56)	• **Hi-Lo/EDLP/EDFP+** *as pricing strategy* • **Store** level • **Multi-dimensional** approach (price /service/assortment)	• "This strategy **(EDLP**, note from the authors) is typically characterized by retail prices, stabilized on an everyday basis, at a level in between the regular and discount prices of promotional retailers." • "The **promotional retailer** sets a low promotional price and a high regular price." • "Typically, EDLP is **accompanied by advertising claims** such as 'guaranteed low prices'." • "Converting profitably to a credible EDLP strategy may be very difficult for a historical HiLo retailer for a variety of reasons. We suggest an alternative means of price stabilization **EDFP+ (everyday fair pricing plus).** EDFP+ means three things: restoration of everyday prices to levels that represent good value to consumers [...]; fewer sales events and **excellence in other differentiating factors of the marketing mix**, such as **service** and **assortment**."
Pechtl 2004 (p. 223-224)	• **Hi-Lo/EDLP** *as pricing strategy* • **Store** level • **One-dimensional** approach	• "In the **high-low promotion strategy (HILO)**, temporary price discounts for selected items occur for some days, followed by weeks with normal prices. In the **every-day-low-price (ELDP) strategy**, the retailer **promotes** a basket of products with the argument to offer attractive low prices with will be constant for a longer period. These prices are lower than normal prices in HILO stores, but not as low as their price discounts."
Popkowski Leszczyc et al. 2004 (p. 86)	• **Hi-Lo/EDLP** as *price format* and **continuum** • **Store** level • **One-dimensional** approach	• "**EDLP** stores tend to offer lower average prices, while **Hi-Lo** stores offer frequent price specials on individual goods. It is more appropriate to view these strategies as **two extreme points on a continuum** as most EDLP stores engage in some price promotions."
Shankar and Bolton 2004	• **Five pricing strategies** (see	• "Third retailer pricing strategy has been typically viewed as one-dimensional. We

Author(s) Year (Page)	Aspects	Definition
(p. 31)	Bolton/Shankar 2003) • **Brand-store** level • **Multi-dimensional** approach (price/promotion)	consider retailers' strategic pricing strategy on **multiple dimensions** that recognize the existence of price promotions."
Shankar and Krishnamurthi 1996 (p. 250)	• **Hi-Lo/EDLP** as *pricing policy with tactical decisions* • **Store** level • **Multi-dimensional** approach (price/promotion)	• "Typically, retailers are faced with two alternative pricing policies, an **Everyday Low Pricing (EDLP)** policy or a **High-Low Pricing (HLP)** policy. Tactical decisions include decisions on retailer promotional variables such as **price cut, feature advertising, and display**."
Tang et al. 2001 (p. 56)	• **Hi-Lo/EDLP** as *retail price format* and **continuum** • **Store** level • **One-dimensional** approach	• "Managers can select a retail price format on a **continuum** anchored by **EDLP** on one end and **HiLo** at the other"
Tsiros and Hardesty 2010 (p. 49)	• **Hi-Lo/EDLP** as *pricing tactic* • **Store** level • **One-dimensional** approach	• "Two particularly popular price promotion tactics are **everyday low pricing (EDLP)** and **hi-lo pricing**. Sellers that employ an EDLP tactic charge a constant, everyday price with no […] temporary price promotions […]. Sellers that employ a hi-lo pricing tactic set relatively higher prices on an everyday basis but offer frequent and substantial price promotions."
Voss and Seiders 2003 (p. 37-38)	• **Price promotion strategy** • **Store** level • **Multi-dimensional** approach (price/promotion)	• "[…] **price promotion strategy**, which we define as a **coordinated set of pricing and promotion decisions** designed to communicate a price position to consumers and influence short-term sales response and overall market performance" • "[…] we examine **three** distinct and important **components of price promotion strategy**: Price variation policy […], Price promotion advertising volume […], Depth of discount […]"

2.4 Review of the research on pricing strategy in retailing

In the following chapter a review of the research on the topic of pricing strategy in retailing is given. We thereby focus on articles that directly relate determinants and outcomes to a certain retail pricing strategy and include both papers with the retailer's and the customer's perspective on pricing strategy in retailing. Single factors could have either been seen as a determinant or an outcome of pricing strategy in retailing. These factors were allocated to one of both groups regarding their content and central findings.

It first makes sense to differentiate between conceptual and empirical papers. Furthermore, the relevant literature can be differentiated in terms of whether the determinants or outcomes of pricing strategy in retailing were examined. For the empirical papers, we follow this division and present the results for both groups separately. For the conceptual papers we present the results without this division as there are just six relevant articles which have different focuses. Finally for the empirical papers, main and further results are discussed. For the conceptual papers this separation was also not possible for the same reason already mentioned. The following figure clarifies the procedure of our systematization of the literature on pricing strategy in retailing.

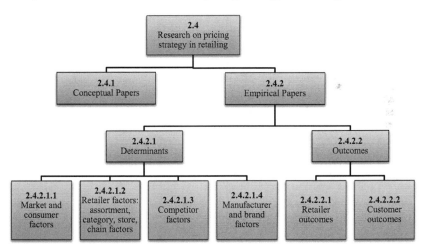

Figure 2:   Systematization of the scientific literature on pricing strategy in retailing

2.4.1 Results of conceptual papers

We found three conceptual papers that investigated the topic of pricing strategy in retailing with regard to determinants and outcomes.

Ortmeyer et al. (1991) discussed the *determinants, benefits and risks* of a change from Hi-Lo strategy to EDLP or EDFP+ (explained in table 1) strategy. Concerning the determinants, they first stated that *younger customers* and dual income-households and *higher income households* prefer EDLP or EDFP+ retailers with a bigger product assortment and exceptional service (p. 58). Second, they asserted that *cherry pickers* – often including *retired persons* and *two-parent families* with one working spouse – will rather choose a Hi-Lo store, whereas the *time-constrained shoppers* rather shop at the EDLP retailer (p. 58; 60). Third, they stated that carrying *easily comparable products* and *frequently purchased products* and having *lower merchandise prices* increases EDLP believability. In contrast, the higher the *amount of fashion merchandise*, the lower is the ability to implement EDLP successfully. Fourth they suggest that retailers with *incomplete assortments* have lower merchandise costs and can therefore offer lower prices to the consumers (p. 59). Finally, the *retailer type* also influences the ability to implement EDLP or EDFP+. Warehouse clubs such as Price Club or Costco can easily implement EDLP "because their prices are both consistently and sufficiently low enough […]" (p. 59). Other retailer types such as grocery stores, category specialists such as Toys R Us and Home Depot, general merchandisers like Sears and traditional department stores like Macys, have more difficulty to promote EDLP as their main competitive advantage because they don't have the lowest prices. Grocery stores have to provide "superior assortments in all departments, exceptional quality in their high-margin perishable departments, and fast and pleasant assistance in service departments and at the check-out counter as further sources of differentiation" (p. 60). As benefits of a strategy change to EDLP or EDFP+ they identified a *smoother demand* (less forecasting error and fewer stock-outs, less customer dissatisfaction, lower administrative costs) and *fewer residuals*, more *efficient inventory management*, more *efficient use of personnel* (reduced personnel costs, more time spent with customer), more *advertising flexibility* (less weekly flyers, more image-related advertising) and more *consumer appeal* (one-stop-shopping, pricing strategy perceived as more honest) (p. 57). As a risk for this strategy change they stated that "*consumers' pricing perceptions* have been conditioned by past pricing practices and may be hard to change […]" (p. 62). A further risk is the possibility of an *erupting price war* due to an aggressive adoption of EDLP. Therefore a change in pricing strategy is expected to lead to a substantial decline in retailer profits, resulting of lower gross margins and higher advertising costs (p. 62).

Kopalle et al. (2009) provided an overall framework of *retailer pricing* and its *competitive effects*. The authors used the terms "pricing strategies", "retailer pricing" and "pricing" as synonyms (cf. Kopalle et al. 2009, p. 56-57). They identified seven different factors that determine retailer pricing – in-channel competition (on product/brand level), cross-channel competition and store positioning/format (EDLP/Hi-Lo), other marketing mix variables, customer factors, product type & complementary, manufacturer interaction and medium (on-/offline) – and derived avenues for future research for each effect.

Similarly, Gauri et al. (2010) presented a conceptual framework of online and offline retail pricing. Thereby the authors focused mostly on papers on tactical pricing instruments. They identified firm factors (retail mix, price format, subscription vs. transaction), product and service characteristics (digital products, product from bundles, commodity information products, custom information products, products vs. services) and channel characteristics (online vs. offline) as key determinants of multi-channel retail pricing. Furthermore, customer characteristics (preference, price sensitivity, price expectation), environmental and economic factors (e.g. recession) and competitive factors (price dispersion, online vs. offline outlets) were identified as moderators of the relation between determinants and pricing strategy. For each determinant and moderator directions for future research were depicted.

There are three further conceptual papers by Levy et al. (2004), Grewal and Levy (2007) and Ailawadi et al. (2009) that center the topics of pricing and retailing, but without specifically focusing on pricing strategy.

Levy et al. (2004) focused in their paper on the *determinants* of *optimal prices* rather than pricing strategy in retailing. They identified seven factors that have to be considered to determine optimal prices in retailing: "(1) *price sensitivity* or how demand for an SKU changes with its price; [...] (2) *substitution effects*, namely how demand for an SKU changes with the price of a competing SKU; (3) *dynamic effect* of price promotions over time, or how changing prices today affects tomorrow's demand; (4) *segment-based pricing*, which investigates how prices vary across different market/customer segments; (5) *cross-category effects*, or accounting for demand complementarities across categories; (6) *retailer costs* (wholesale prices and trade deals) and *discounts*; and (7) to what extent *competition* at the retail level influences retail prices." (Levy et al. 2004, p. 16).

Grewal/Levy (2007) reviewed all papers published in the Journal of Retailing between 2002 and 2007 and classified them into the following ten broad topic categories: price, promotion, brand/product, service, loyalty, consumer behavior, channel, organizational, internet and other. Then they highlighted key insights and derived avenues for future research for each area.

Ailawadi et al. (2009, p. 42) built a conceptual framework with the relationships between *manufacturer and retailer decisions* on communication and promotion and *retailer performance*, with focus on the retailer's perspective. The authors examined single retailer decisions on price promotion, non-price support, price, advertising, loyalty program and national brand vs. private label and derived avenues for future research. The objectives of the retailer are to maximize corporate, chain, store, category, private label and customer profits. Thereby the outcome measures are store traffic, sales per square foot, store share, profit, store satisfaction and share of wallet (cf. Ailawadi et al. 2009, p. 44). Concerning their literature review in the field of consumer promotions, the authors stated that "retailers can improve the effectiveness of promotions by coordinating them with pricing decisions. They can use the knowledge and understanding of the determinants of price promotion strategy and coordination to improve their profitability." (Ailawadi et al. 2009, p. 49). With respect to future research the authors claim more research from the retailer's point of view as there is already much research from the manufacturer's perspective (cf. Ailawadi et al. 2009, p. 50).

2.4.2 Results of empirical papers

2.4.2.1 Determinants of pricing strategy in retailing

Previous research distinguished between several determinants of pricing strategy in retailing such as customer factors, market factors, chain factors, store factors, category factors, brand factors, competitor factors and assortment factors. Based on our intensive literature review, we decided to allocate some determinants shown in previous research because they are strongly related concerning the content. Therefore we build four groups of determinants of pricing strategy in retailing – market and consumer factors, retailer factors (assortment, category, store and chain factors), competitor factors and manufacturer and brand factors – and present the results for each group separately.

2.4.2.1.1   *Market and consumer factors*

Table 2 shows the papers that examined the influence of market and consumer factors on the pricing strategy in retailing and summarizes the central findings. The table also shows the specific determinants/independent variables and the dependent variables in the single papers.

Main results

In general, Ellickson and Misra (2008, p. 812) found that consumer demographics are very important in the choice of pricing strategies. Retailers choose the pricing strategy that their consumers demand. Also Gauri et al. (2008, p. 258) mention that the characteristics of the trading area such as population density, income, distance from store and other sociodemographic variables are important for the choice of pricing and format strategy of retailers.

The first converging result within the group "market and consumer factors" deals with the influence of *consumer income* on pricing strategy in retailing. Ellickson and Misra (2008, p. 812) found that consumer demographics are very important in the choice of pricing strategies. Retailers choose the pricing strategy that their consumers demand. They found that consumers with lower income prefer EDLP, whereas consumers with higher income clearly prefer Hi-Lo. This finding is consistent with the research of Bell et al. (1998, p. 365) who found that lower income families prefer EDLP. Also Gauri et al. (2008, p. 263) found that "as the average income [...] in the trading area increases, retailers also prefer a HiLo or hybrid pricing strategy". Bailey (2008, p. 218) also expected higher income consumers to be less price sensitive and therefore less responsive to EDLP, but – in contrast to the above shown results – discovered that consumer income has no significant impact on consumer attitude toward EDLP. As an explanation they state "that consumers, regardless of income levels, like to shop around for deals" (Bailey 2008, p. 219). In contrast to these results, Popkowski Leszczyc et al. (2000, p. 339) as well as Popkowski Leszczyc et al. (2004, p. 93) found no significant influence of family income on store choice.

The second converging result for market and consumer factors covers the influence of *family size* on pricing strategy in retailing. Bell et al. (1998, p. 365) as well as Ellickson and Misra (2008, p. 815) stated that larger families prefer EDLP stores. On the other hand, Gauri et al. (2008, p. 263) asserted that household size doesn't have a significant impact on the pricing strategy. Also Pechtl (2004, p. 228) didn't find a significant difference between EDLP and Hi-Lo prone shoppers with regard to family or household size. Popkowski Leszczyc et al. (2000, p. 339) even found that household size has the strongest positive effect on the likelihood of a shopping trip for the consumer segment which rather shops at Hi-Lo stores.

One of the most researched and largely discussed determinants of pricing strategy in retailing is the *size of the shopping basket*. This is the third converging result found in existing relevant literature. Bell and Lattin (1998, p. 66) detected that large basket shoppers prefer EDLP, whereas small basket shoppers prefer Hi-Lo. This result is also echoed by Bell et al. (1998, p. 365-366) who found that large basket shoppers prefer stores with higher fixed and lower variable costs which they equalize with EDLP stores. Further support for this result is drawn from Pechtl (2004, p. 229) who stated that EDLP prone consumers tend to have larger shopping baskets. Furthermore, Tang et al. (2001, p. 63) asserted that large basket shoppers perceive a higher total utility (fixed and variable utility, benefits-costs) at EDLP stores and that small basket shoppers perceive a higher total utility at Hi-Lo stores.

The fourth converging result deals with the influence of *population density* on pricing strategy in retailing. Gauri et al. (2008, p. 263) stated that populous neighborhoods are more associated with Hi-Lo or hybrid pricing strategy than with EDLP. Shankar and Bolton (2004) postulated that the fact, "whether the market is a metropolitan city or a small city, may be associated with a particular pricing environment and thus may be related to pricing practice" (p. 34). They looked at the influence of the market type "metropolitan city vs. small city" on the four underlying dimensions of retailer pricing strategy – price consistency, price promotion intensity, price promotion coordination and relative brand price – and not on the pricing strategy as a construct. Therefore it is difficult to clearly relate a determinant to a certain pricing strategy. They found that „retailers in metropolitan cities tend to be more price consistent than those in smaller cities" (p. 38), which is intuitively rather a sign for EDLP than for Hi-Lo. Furthermore, a "retailer tends to coordinate price and promotion when the store is located in metropolitan cities" (p. 40). The type of market (metropolitan or small city) doesn't have an impact on promotion intensity and relative brand price. According to the classification scheme of Bolton and Shankar (2003, p. 220), these results could also be interpreted as a Hi-Lo pricing strategy.

The fifth determinant found in the relevant literature is about the influence of *shopping frequency* on pricing strategy in retailing. Bell and Lattin (1998, p. 93) found that consumers who shop more frequently prefer Hi-Lo stores, whereas shoppers who shop less frequently prefer EDLP stores. This finding was supported by Popkowski Leszczyc et al. (2000, p. 339) and Popkowski Leszczyc et al. (2004, p. 93) who stated that the shopping frequency is higher for the consumer segment that rather shops at Hi-Lo stores.

The sixth important determinant within this group is the *segmentation of customers into time constrained service or price seekers, expected price-shoppers and cherry pickers*. Cherry pickers are actively searching for price promotions and willing to shop opportunistically and accelerate the purchase when a better price comes available. The expected price shopper wants to shop at a reasonable price but doesn't want "to spent time monitoring day to day price changes or time their purchases during the retailer's deal interval"

(Lattin/Ortmeyer 1991, p. 4). The time constrained shoppers have high opportunity costs for shopping (Popkowski Leszczyc et al. 2004, p. 88). Lattin and Ortmeyer (1991, p. 62) affirmed that EDLP appeals the expected-price shoppers and the Hi-Lo retailer can price discriminate between cherry pickers and the expected-price shoppers. Lal and Rao (1997, p. 62) stated that EDLP stores attract time constrained customers, whereas Hi-Lo attracts the cherry pickers. When service is included, Hi-Lo stores offer a higher service level to attract time constrained consumers, whereas EDLP stores offer a lower service level and attract cherry pickers. In contrast to the finding of Lattin and Ortmeyer (1991), they found that both EDLP and Hi-Lo stores attract both types of customers. In accordance with Lal and Rao (1997), Popkowski Leszczyc et al. (2004, p. 89) assert that EDLP stores attract the time constrained price seekers and that time constrained service seekers prefer to shop at Hi-Lo stores. Furthermore they also found that cherry pickers don't have a certain preference for a specific store for their grocery purchases and therefore shop at both EDLP and Hi-Lo stores. The seventh converging determinant is the *price sensitivity of consumers*. Shankar and Bolton (2004, p. 39) investigated the impact of own-/cross-price and deal elasticity on the four dimensions of pricing strategy in retailing, as described above. They found that these elasticities "explain only a small portion of the variance in retailer pricing, but they are significant" (Shankar/Bolton 2004, p. 44). In general they stated that in own-price elastic markets, retailers tend to use price rather than promotions as their primary marketing tool. On the other hand, in more deal-elastic markets, retailers tend to use promotions rather than price changes as their primary marketing tool (cf. Shankar/Bolton 2004, p. 44). These results are in line with the study of Shankar and Krishnamurthi (1996, p. 269), who found that EDLP stores attract more price-sensitive shoppers compared to Hi-Lo, whereas Hi-Lo stores attract more deal-sensitive consumers.

The *sale proneness* and *store loyalty* of consumers are two further determinants examined in the context of pricing strategy in retailing. Pechtl (2004, p. 224; 231) stated that EDLP prone consumers prefer EDLP stores and Hi-Lo prone consumers prefer Hi-Lo stores. But as stronger differences could have been expected, they derived that both consumer types also buy in both store types. Bailey (2008, p. 215) examined the influence of sale proneness and store loyalty on consumer response to EDLP. It was discovered that high sale-prone consumers respond more favorably to EDLP than low sale-prone consumers. Furthermore, customers who are loyal are less responsive to an EDLP announcement by a competitor. According to the authors, when implementing an EDLP strategy, retailers can segment the market according to the sale proneness of the consumers. Similarly, Hoch et al. (1994, p. 23) affirmed that the greater the installed base, the more difficult it will be to make EDLP pay out. The installed base consists of consumers already shopping at the retailer. Kocas and Bohlmann (2008, p. 124; 138) stated that the pricing strategy of a retailer to discount deeply or frequently is driven by the ratio of the size of switcher segments for which the retailer competes to the size of its loyal segment. Rather in contrast to Hoch et al. (1994) they stated, that a large retailer should offer deeper (shallower) discounts than a smaller firm if the relative share of switchers is large (small).

The tenth and last identified converging result addresses the influence of *fixed and variable costs and utility* on pricing strategy in retailing. Tang et al. (2001, p. 58) affirmed that a customer's choice of store depends on the perceived fixed and variable utility from that store, e.g. benefits minus costs. "The perceived fixed utility does not vary from trip to trip and is not a function of the shopping list [...] the perceived variable utility changes from trip to trip because it depends on the size and composition of the shopping list" (Tang et al. 2008, p. 58). They found that Hi-Lo stores have a higher fixed utility and a lower variable utility than EDLP stores. These results are in line with the study of Bell et al. (1998, p. 366) who found out that EDLP stores impose higher average fixed costs and lower average variable costs and that large basket shoppers prefer stores with higher fixed and lower variable costs, hence EDLP stores.

Table 2: Empirical research on the influence of market and consumer factors on pricing strategy in retailing

Author(s) Year (Journal)	Methodology	Sample (N)	Determinant(s) / Independent Variable(s)	Dependent Variable(s)	Central Findings
Bailey 2008 (JRCS) C	• Grocery industry Study • Study 1 (Experiment): ANOVA • Study 2 (survey): Multiple regression analysis	$N_1 = 86$ students $N_2 = 181$ students	**Consumer factors:** • Sale proneness • Store loyalty • Consumer income	Consumer response to EDLP = Attitude toward EDLP, attitude toward the chain, store patronage intentions	• High sale-prone consumers respond more favorably to a new EDLP policy than low sale-prone consumers • High store-loyal consumers will exhibit lower likelihood of patronage of a competing retailer implementing EDLP than low store-loyal consumers • Consumer income has no impact on consumer attitude toward EDLP • Consumer income has an impact on consumer attitude toward a retailer implementing EDLP and on consumer intentions to patronize a retailer that implements EDLP • Marketers can use sale proneness as a segmentation variable when implementing EDLP
Bell et al. 1998 (JMR) C	• Scanner panel data • 2 years (1991-1993) • Shopping behavior at 5 supermarkets, 943 SKUs • Metropolitan area in US	$N = 520$ households	**Market/Consumer factors:** • Fixed and variable costs of shopping • Family size • Age • Income • Large and small basket	Store choice (EDLP or Hi-Lo)	• EDLP stores impose higher average fixed costs and lower average variable costs • Large basket shoppers prefer stores with higher fixed and lower variable costs → EDLP, Small basket shoppers prefer Hi-Lo stores • Larger, younger families with lower income prefer EDLP stores • Focus strategy: serve small (large) basket sizes in all market segments with smallest (largest) fixed and highest (smallest) variable cost of

Author(s) Year (Journal)	Methodology	Sample (N)	Determinant(s) / Independent Variable(s)	Dependent Variable(s)	Central Findings
	• Logit model		shoppers		shopping • Diversified strategy: serve large basket sizes in some segments and small basket sizes in others • Both strategies can lead to gains in store traffic at the expense of competitors
Bell and Lattin 1998 (MS) C	• Supermarket industry • Scanner panel data • 12 categories • 104 weeks (1991-1993) • Markets A,B • Logit model	$N_A = 484$ households $N_B = 548$ households	**Consumer factors:** • Expected basket attractiveness • Large and small basket shopper • Shopping frequency	Store choice (EDLP or Hi-Lo)	• Price expectations for the basket influence store choice • Large basket shoppers prefer EDLP stores • Small basket shoppers prefer Hi-Lo stores • Households who shop more frequently prefer Hi-Lo • Households who shop less frequently prefer EDLP
Ellickson and Misra 2008 (MS) R	• Supermarket store level data (1998) • Discrete choice models	N = every super-market operating in the U.S.	**Market/Consumer factors:** • Household income • Family size • Median vehicle ownership • Racial composition	Pricing strategy (EDLP, Hi-Lo)	• EDLP is the preferred strategy for geographic markets that have larger households, more racial diversity, lower income and fewer vehicles per household → EDLP is mostly aimed at lower income consumers with large families, i.e. more urbanized areas • Consumers with higher income prefer Hi-Lo
Gauri et al. 2008 (JR)	• Grocery industry	N = 3297 grocery	**Market/Consumer factors:**	Retail Strategy	• Higher income and populous neighborhoods are more associated with Hi-Lo or hybrid pricing

Author(s) Year (Journal)	Methodology	Sample (N)	Determinant(s) / Independent Variable(s)	Dependent Variable(s)	Central Findings
R	• Secondary data (2003 and 2000) • Multinominal logit model	stores from 66 chains (New York, Pennsylvania, Ohio)	• Income • Household size • Age • Population density	(=pricing and format strategy)	strategy than with EDLP • Household size and age don't have a significant impact on the pricing strategy
Hoch et al. 1994 (JM) R	• Supermarket industry • Experiments • Study 1: 19 categories • Study 2: 26 categories • Study 3: 18 categories	N = 86 stores (1 retailer)	**Consumer factors:** • Installed base of current users and nonusers	EDLP	• In executing any pricing strategy, firms must consider the likely impact on two consumer sectors: their installed base of current users and nonusers who represent potential opportunity for growth • Installed base consists of consumers already shopping at one of the locations of the retailer • The profit potential of EDLP depends on large part on the ratio of installed base to new opportunity. The greater the installed base, the more difficult it will be to make EDLP pay out.
Kocas and Bohlmann 2008 (JM) R	• Online book retailers • Regression analysis, tests of stochastic dominance • Study 1: descriptive data • Study 2: panel	N = 1640 books N = 100,000 panelists	**Consumer factors:** • Size of switcher segments	Retailer pricing strategies (strategy to discount deeply or frequently)	• Retailer's strategy to discount deeply or frequently is driven by the ratio of the size of switcher segments for which the retailer competes to its loyal segment size • A large retailer should offer deeper (shallower) discounts than a smaller firm if the relative share of switchers is large (small) • A midsize retailer should follow a partitioned discounting strategy (combination of frequent shallow and infrequent deep or infrequent

Author(s) Year (Journal)	Methodology	Sample (N)	Determinant(s) / Independent Variable(s)	Dependent Variable(s)	Central Findings
	data: internet browsing and purchase data for 100,000 panelists				shallow and frequent deep) discounts → competition at multiple fronts • A small retailer should price high and play the niche and can sometimes benefit from strategically limiting its access to switchers to soften price competition
Lal and Rao 1997 (MS) R	• Supermarket industry • Game theoretic analysis	N = 2 supermarkets each with 2 products	**Consumer factors:** • Time constrained consumers • Cherry pickers	Pricing Strategies (EDLP, Hi-Lo)	• The EDLP stores attract time constrained consumers and the Hi-Lo stores attract cherry pickers • When service is incorporated, Hi-Lo stores offer a higher service level to attract time constrained consumers • EDLP stores offer a lower service level and attract cherry pickers • Both formats attract both kind of customers
Lattin and Ortmeyer 1991 (research paper) R	• Grocery industry • Game theoretic model	N = 2 retailers, 1 product, 2 customer types (less price sensitive, price sensitive)	**Consumer factors:** • Cherry pickers • Expected-price shoppers	Pricing strategies (EDLP, Hi-Lo)	• Retailers use different pricing strategies to segment the market and consumers self-select based on their shopping behavior • Grocery stores compete for two types of consumers: cherry pickers and expected-price shoppers • The EDLP appeals the expected-price shoppers • The Hi-Lo retailer is able to price discriminate between the cherry pickers and the expected-price shoppers
Pechtl 2004 (JRCS)	• Interviews in 2 large	N = 620 shoppers	**Consumer factors:**	Store choice (EDLP or	• EDLP prone consumers tend to prefer EDLP stores and have larger shopping baskets than

Author(s) Year (Journal)	Methodology	Sample (N)	Determinant(s) / Independent Variable(s)	Dependent Variable(s)	Central Findings
C	grocery stores in Germany (2000) • Cluster Analysis, T-Test, ANOVA		• Gender • Age • Household size • Size of shopping basket • EDLP prone consumers • Hi-Lo prone consumers	Hi-Lo)	other segments, Hi-Lo prone consumers tend to prefer Hi-Lo stores. But both consumer types also buy in both EDLP and Hi-Lo stores → stronger differences could have been expected • Deal prone segments differ in gender and age (age: small differences), but not in household size • Females tend to be either non-deal or Hi-Lo prone
Popkowski Leszczyc et al. 2000 (JR) C	• Scanner panel data • 21 grocery stores, 5 different store chains in Springfield, Missouri • 3 years (1986-1988) • Hazard Model	N = 169661 shopping trips for 1367 households N_{sub} = 29743 shopping trips for 167 households	• Household size • Family income • Shopping frequency • Hours worked • Amount spent per trip	Store choice (EDLP, Hi-Lo)	• All demographic variables are significant except from family income • The number of hours worked by a household decreases the likelihood of shopping trips for segment 1(rather EDLP) but increases the likelihood for segment 2 (rather Hi-Lo). Segment 2 consists of more single earner families with a stay-at-home spouse who has more time to go shopping • The shopping frequency is greatest for segment two (rather Hi-Lo) • Households that spend more per shopping trip tend to shop less often, particularly for households in segment 1 (rather EDLP) • Household size has a positive effect on the likelihood of a shopping trip. This effect is the

Author(s) Year (Journal)	Methodology	Sample (N)	Determinant(s) / Independent Variable(s)	Dependent Variable(s)	Central Findings
					strongest for segment 2 (rather Hi-Lo)
Popkowski Leszczyc et al. 2004 (JR) C	• Data on shopping behavior 13 grocery stores, 5 chains, 858 observations • Factor analytical latent class logit model	N = 200 respondents	**Consumer factors:** • Shopping frequency • Income • Household size • Weekly expenditures • Time-constrained service seekers • Time-constrained price seekers • Cherry pickers	"Pricing strategy" (shop at EDLP or Hi-Lo), location strategy, shopping strategy (single-purpose or multi-purpose shopping trips)	• The shopping frequency has a negative impact on store chain choice for EDLP shoppers but a positive effect for Hi-Lo shoppers → households shopping at EDLP stores shop less often • Household size has a positive impact on store choice • Income and weekly expenditures don't have a significant impact on store choice • The time-constrained service seekers like to shop at Hi-Lo stores with higher service and convenient locations close to the households • The time-constrained price seekers like to shop at EDLP stores, where they obtain lower average prices. Travel distance is not that important and these households tend to buy larger quantities and make fewer shopping trips • The cherry pickers has a low opportunity cost for shopping and they shop at more than one store in order to search for the best prices. Hence travel distance is less important.
Shankar and Bolton 2004 (MS) R	• Supermarket scanner data • 6 categories • 2 years • SEM model	N = 1364 brand-store combinations	**Market factors:** • Market type (metro/small city)	Retailer pricing strategy (single dimensions)	• Retailers in metropolitan cities tend to be more **price consistent** than those in smaller cities. • Market type doesn't have a significant impact on **promotion intensity** and **relative brand price**

Author(s) Year (Journal)	Methodology	Sample (N)	Determinant(s) / Independent Variable(s)	Dependent Variable(s)	Central Findings
			Consumer factors: • Own-price elasticities • Cross-price elasticities • Deal elasticities		• In metropolitan cities, retailers tend to **coordinate price and promotion** • **Prices** are **more consistent, price promotion** is **less intensive** and **less coordinated** and **relative brand prices** are **lower** for brands in markets that are **own-price elastic** → retailers will tend to use price rather than deal activity as their primary competitive marketing tool in these markets • **Prices** are **inconsistent, price promotion** is **more intensive** and **less coordinated** and **relative brand prices** are **higher** in markets that are more **deal-elastic**. → retailers tend to use promotions rather than price changes as their competitive marketing tool in these markets
Shankar and Krishnamurthi 1996 (JR) **R**	• Store-level data for leading brand-size of mouthwash (low involvement supermarket category) • 104 weekly observations • Top 2 chains	EDLP-Chain: N = 20 stores Hi-Lo-Chain: N = 18 stores	**Consumer factors:** • Price sensitivity	Retailer promotional variables, Pricing policy (EDLP, Hi-Lo)	• An EDLP chain attracts more price sensitive consumers, contributing to the higher level of regular price elasticity in the chain. • A Hi-Lo chain draws consumers who are not as price sensitive as those of the EDLP chain → lower regular price elasticity in the Hi-Lo stores. • Hi-Lo stores attract more deal-sensitive consumers ("cherry pickers")

Author(s) Year (Journal)	Methodology	Sample (N)	Determinant(s) / Independent Variable(s)	Dependent Variable(s)	Central Findings
	for analysis • Multistage regression analysis				
Tang et al. 2001 (CMR) C	• Basket of 12 highest-selling items from 12 categories, 3000 SKUs • 5 supermarkets, Chicago • 2 years • Logit model	N >500 households	**Consumer factors:** • Fixed and variable utility (benefits-costs) • Large and small basket shoppers	Store choice (EDLP or Hi-Lo)	• Hi-Lo stores have a higher fixed, but lower variable utility than EDLP stores • Large basket shoppers perceive a higher total utility at EDLP stores • Hi-Lo stores have higher fixed and lower variable utility • Small basket shoppers perceive a higher total utility at Hi-Lo stores

C = Customer's Perspective of the Paper, R = Retailer's Perspective of the Paper; CMR = California Management Review, JR = Journal of Retailing, JBR = Journal of Business Research, JM = Journal of Marketing, JRCS = Journal of Retailing and Consumer Services, MS = Marketing Science, QME = Quantitative Marketing and Economics

Further results

Besides the above shown results, we found six further determinants of pricing strategy in retailing in the group "market and consumer factors", but which cannot be aggregated to converging or diverging results: age, gender median vehicle ownership, racial composition, number of hours worked and amount spent per trip.

Concerning the influence of *age* of customers on pricing strategy in retailing, Bell et al. (1998, p. 365) found that younger customers prefer EDLP stores. In contrast, Gauri et al. (2008, p. 259; 263) couldn't confirm their hypothesis that older age level customers are associated with Hi-Lo. Pechtl (2004, p. 228) found just small, no substantial differences between EDLP and Hi-Lo prone consumers regarding age and therefore stated that age will not help to segment shoppers according to their deal proneness to an EDLP or Hi-Lo strategy. Pechtl (2004, p. 228; 230) stated that deal prone segments also differ in *gender*. He found a higher proportion of males among the EDLP prone consumers and a higher proportion of females among the Hi-Lo and non-deal prone consumers. Ellickson and Misra (2008, p. 823) used *median vehicle ownership* and *racial composition* as determinants of pricing strategy in retailing and stated that EDLP is the preferred strategy for geographic markets that have more racial diversity and fewer vehicles per household. Popkowski Leszczyc et al. (2000, p. 339) stated that the *number of hours worked* by a household decreases the likelihood of shopping trips for the consumer segment that shops at EDLP, but increases the likelihood for the consumer segment that shops at Hi-Lo stores. They assume that the Hi-Lo segment consists "of more single earner families with a stay-at-home spouse who has more time to go shopping" (Popkowski Leszczyc et al. 2000, p. 339). Another determinant they investigated was the *amount spent per trip*. They assert that households that spend more per shopping trip tend to shop less often, particularly for households rather shopping at EDLP stores. In contrast, Popkowski Leszczyc et al. (2004, p. 93) stated that weekly expenditures don't have a significant impact on store choice.

2.4.2.1.2   Retailer factors

Table 3 shows the results of the literature analysis. The most important results are aggregated below.

Main results

The first converging result (subgroup "store factors") deals with the influence of *store size* on pricing strategy in retailing. Popkowski Leszczyc et al. (2000, p. 339) found that larger stores are associated with EDLP, whereas smaller stores are more likely to apply a Hi-Lo strategy. Similarly, Voss and Seiders (2003, p. 45) asserted that firms with smaller stores use more price variation, whereas retailers with larger stores rather promote stable everyday prices. Furthermore, retailers with smaller stores promote their prices less likely and tend to offer deeper discounts than retailers with larger stores. Ellickson and Misra (2008, p. 822) also stated that EDLP is the preferred strategy of retailers with larger stores. Shankar and Bolton (2004, p. 38-42) detected different results and stated that larger stores are associated with higher price promotion intensity and price promotion coordination and lower relative brand price. According to Bolton and Shankar (2003, p. 220) this results can be equalized with a Hi-Lo pricing strategy on the store level.

The second converging result (subgroup "chain factors") discusses the influence of chain size, the number of stores in a chain, on pricing strategy in retailing. Shankar and Bolton (2004, p. 38-42) found that smaller chains are associated with higher price consistency, lower price promotion intensity and lower price promotion coordination which can be equalized with "Exclusive pricing" or "Low pricing" (cf. Bolton/Shankar 2003, p. 220). In line with this result, Ellickson and Misra (2008, p. 823) affirmed that "the total number of stores in the chain is negatively related to EDLP". Voss and Seiders (2003, p. 45) discovered differentiated results and stated that smaller chains promote their prices less likely and offer deeper discounts than larger chains. The fact to promote less likely is rather a sign for EDLP, but the fact to offer deeper discounts is rather a sign for Hi-Lo.

Table 3:   Empirical research on the influence of retailer factors (assortment, category, store, chain factors) on pricing strategy in retailing

Author(s) Year (Journal)	Methodology	Sample (N)	Determinant(s) / Independent Variable(s)	Dependent Variable(s)	Central Findings
Ellickson and Misra 2008 (MS) R	• Supermarket store level data (1998) • Discrete choice models	N=every supermarket operating in the U.S.	**Store factors:** • Store size • Vertically integrated **Chain factors:** • Number of stores in chain • Chain effect • Chain/global market effect	Pricing strategy (EDLP, Hi-Lo)	• Stores choosing EDLP are both significantly larger and far more likely to be vertically integrated into distribution → EDLP requires substantial firm level investment, careful inventory management and a deeper selection of products in each store in order to satisfy the demands of one-stop shoppers • Pricing strategy involves developing an overall positioning strategy, requiring complementary investments in store quality and product selection • The total number of stores in the chain is negatively related to EDLP • Chain and chain/global market random effects are highly significant
Gauri et al. 2008 (JR) R	• Grocery industry, secondary data (2003,2000) • Multinominal logit model	N=3297 grocery stores from 66 chains (New York, Pennsylvania, Ohio)	**Store factors:** • Number of features/ services	Retail strategy (=pricing and format strategy)	• Improved service features are more associated with Hi-Lo or hybrid pricing than with EDLP pricing strategies
Popkowski Leszczyc et al. 2000 (JR)	• Scanner panel data • 21 grocery stores, 5	N=16966 1 shopping trips,	**Store factors:** • Store size	Store choice (EDLP, Hi-Lo)	• Households in segment 1 tend to shop in larger stores that are rather located in suburban areas and are more likely to apply an EDLP strategy (p. 339) • Households in segment 2 tend to shop in smaller stores that

Author(s) Year (Journal)	Methodology	Sample (N)	Determinant(s) / Independent Variable(s)	Dependent Variable(s)	Central Findings
C	different store chains in Springfield, Missouri • 3 years (1986-1988)	1367 households $N_{sub}=297$ 43 shopping trips, 167 households			are rather located in neighborhood areas and are more likely to apply a Hi-Lo strategy
Shankar and Bolton 2004 (MS) R	• Supermarket scanner data • 6 categories • 2 years • SEM model	N=1364 brand-store combinations	**Category factors:** • Storability • Necessity • Assortment size **Store/Category factors:** • Store size • Category assortment **Chain factors:** • Chain size • Chain positioning	Retailer pricing strategy (single dimensions)	• Retailers are more **price consistent** for brands in storable categories (e.g. bathroom tissue, bleach), categories that are necessities (e.g. bathroom tissue) and categories with small assortments → retailers may choose to be less consistent for non-storable, nonessential categories • **Price promotion intensity** is high for storable products and for product categories that are necessities • **Price promotion coordination** is lower for storable categories and higher for necessity categories • **(Relative brand price:** insignificant results for storability and necessity) • Retailers are more **price consistent** for smaller chains and those positioned as EDLP chains (chain size and positioning) and for categories with smaller assortments (category assortment; store size is insignificant) • The **price promotion intensity** is higher for larger chains and for Hi-Lo chains, for larger stores and in categories with small numbers of brands • A retailer tends to **coordinate price and promotion** when

Author(s) Year (Journal)	Methodology	Sample (N)	Determinant(s) / Independent Variable(s)	Dependent Variable(s)	Central Findings
					it is part of a large chain or a chain positioned as Hi-Lo, for brands in large stores and with large category assortments • **Relative brand price** is lower for brands in large stores and with large category assortments and for EDLP stores (chain size not significant)
Voss and Seiders 2003 (JR) R	• Supermarket industry • 11 retail sectors • Advertisement tracking for dependent variables • Annual reports (1998) for independent variables • Hierarchical linear modeling (HLM)	N = 38 firms	**Assortment factors:** • Assortment perishability • Assortment heterogenity **Store/Chain factors:** • Retailer differentiation • Store size • Number of stores	Retail price promotion strategy (single dimensions)	• At the retail sector level, product assortment perishability has a positive effect on price variation, price promotion advertising volume and average depth of discount (= three dependent variables) • At the retail sector level, product assortment heterogeneity acts as a quasi-moderator, exerting a direct positive effect on price variation and average depth of discount (no effect on price promotion advertising volume) and exerting a moderating effect on the association between assortment perishability and all dependent variables • For retailer differentiation there are no significant results • At the retail firm level, as the number of stores increases, price promotion advertising volume will increase, average depth of discount will decrease • At the retail firm level, as average store size increases, price variation will decrease, price promotion advertising volume will increase and average depth of discount will decrease

C = Customer's Perspective of the Paper, R = Retailer's Perspective of the Paper; JR = Journal of Retailing, JM = Journal of Marketing, MS = Marketing Science, JRCS = Journal of Retailing and Consumer Services

Further results

Regarding the subgroup "assortment and category factors" we found no converging results in the studied literature and summarize the findings in the following. Shankar and Bolton (2004, p. 38-42) found that *storable categories* are associated with higher price consistency, higher price promotion intensity and lower price promotion coordination (rather "Exclusive pricing" or "Premium pricing" according to Bolton/Shankar 2003, p. 220) whereas *necessary categories* are associated with higher price consistency, higher price promotion intensity and higher price promotion coordination (rather Hi-Lo pricing according to Bolton and Shankar 2003, p. 220). *Smaller assortments* are related to higher price consistency, higher price promotion intensity, higher price promotion coordination and higher relative brand price. Voss and Seiders (2003, p. 46) used *assortment perishability* and *assortment heterogeneity* across competitors as determinants of their identified three dimensions of retail price promotion strategy. Assortment heterogeneity describes the degree of product variability between competing stores in the same retail industry. Assortment perishability can be referred to assortment lifespan and is defined as a function of the speed at which a product loses its value. They found that assortment perishability has a positive direct effect on price variation, price promotion advertising volume and average depth of discount. They further stated that when assortment heterogeneity across retailers is high, "perishability had no effect on price variation, a negative effect on price promotion advertising volume, and a positive effect on average depth of discount" (Voss/Seiders 2003, p. 46). Furthermore, assortment heterogeneity has a positive direct effect on price variation and average depth of discount, but no significant effect on price promotion advertising volume. According to the authors, competitors in heterogeneous sectors should advertise more their assortment rather than their prices. Similar to Shankar and Bolton (2004) one cannot derive clear predictions for the identified determinants of Voss and Seiders (2003) with regard to specific pricing strategies (EDLP, Hi-Lo).

In the subgroup "store factors", Ellickson and Misra (2008) discovered that stores with an EDLP strategy are "far more likely to be *vertically integrated* into distribution" (p. 823) than Hi-Lo or Hybrid stores. Another aspect was mentioned by Gauri et al. (2008, p. 263) who investigated the *number of services in a store* as determinant of pricing strategy. They found that increased service levels are rather associated with Hi-Lo or hybrid pricing strategy than with EDLP.

2.4.2.1.3 Competitor factors

In this subchapter we discuss the competitor factors as determinants of pricing strategy in retailing. In general, competitor factors are claimed by some authors to explain the most variation in retailer pricing strategy. Table 4 gives an overview of the results of the literature analysis.

We found only one converging result in the group of competitor factors which deals with the influence of *competitor pricing strategy* on the retailer's pricing strategy. Shankar and Bolton (2004, p. 33-34) look at *competitor price level* and *competitor deal frequency* as competitor factors. They found that competitor factors are the most dominant determinants of retailer pricing strategy among several other determinants. Ellickson and Misra (2008, p. 815) also stated that competitor factors play a major role in determining retailer pricing strategy.

In detail, when "competitors charge lower prices, a retailer communicates the relative attractiveness of its offerings through higher price consistency, lower price promotion intensity, and higher price promotion coordination – while maintaining lower relative brand prices" (Shankar/Bolton 2004, p. 42). According to Bolton and Shankar (2003, p. 20) this can be equalized with a "low pricing" or "aggressive pricing" strategy at the store level. Furthermore, when "competitors offer deals more frequently, retailers are less price consistent, offer aggressive promotions, more actively coordinate price promotion, and charge lower prices (Shankar/Bolton 2004, p. 43). This can rather be equalized with a Hi-Lo pricing strategy on the store level (cf. Bolton/Shankar 2003, p. 220). These results show that retailers match their own pricing strategy with the competitor's pricing strategy. Ellickson and Misra (2008) asserted that "firms coordinate their actions, choosing pricing strategies that match their rivals (p. 822). More specifically they state, that retailers with a high share of EDLP-competitors will far more likely choose an EDLP than either Hi-Lo or hybrid pricing strategy.

Table 4:   *Empirical research on the influence of competitor factors on pricing strategy in retailing*

Author(s) Year (Journal)	Methodology	Sample (N)	Determinant(s)/Independent Variable(s)	Dependent Variable(s)	Central Findings
Ellickson and Misra 2008 (MS) **R**	• Supermarket store level data (1998) • Discrete choice models	N=every super-market operating in the U.S.	**Competitor factors:** • Rival pricing policies	Pricing strategy (EDLP, Hi-Lo)	• Firms facing competition from many EDLP stores rather choose EDLP than either HYBRID or PROMO • No evidence that firms differentiate themselves with regard to pricing strategy; pricing strategies are strategic complements rather than vehicles for differentiation
Gauri et al. 2008 (JR) **R**	• Grocery industry, secondary data (2003, 2000) • Multinominal logit model	N=3297 grocery stores from 66 chains (New York, Pennsylvania, Ohio)	**Competitor factors:** • Distance to competition • Stores with same strategy in neighborhood	Retail strategy (=pricing and format strategy)	• As the proportion of Hi-Lo stores in a trading area increases, retailers prefer Hi-Lo over EDLP → no differentiation exists • As the proportion of hybrid stores increases, retailers prefer EDLP over a hybrid strategy → differentiation exists • As the average distance to competitors increase, retailers tend to prefer Hi-Lo over EDLP
Shankar and Bolton 2004 (MS) **R**	• Supermarket scanner data • 6 categories • 2 years • SEM model	N=1364 brand-store combinations	**Competitor factors:** • Competitor price level • Competitor deal frequency	Retailer pricing strategy (single dimensions)	• **Price consistency** is higher when competitors' prices are lower and when competitors' deals are less frequent • The higher the competitor price level and deal frequency, the higher is the **price promotion intensity** • **Price promotion coordination** is higher when competitors' prices are lower and competitors' deal frequencies are higher • **Relative brand price** is lower when competitor prices are lower and competitor deals are more frequent.

R = Retailer's Perspective of the Paper; JR = Journal of Retailing, MS = Marketing Science

Therefore there is "no evidence that firms differentiate themselves with regard to pricing strategy" (p. 823). These results are echoed by Gauri et al. (2008) who found that as the number of Hi-Lo stores "in the trading area increases, retailers continue to prefer Hi-Lo over EDLP" (p. 263). In this case, no differentiation in pricing strategy exists, as also stated by Ellickson and Misra (2008). But as the number stores with hybrid pricing strategy increases, retailers prefer EDLP over hybrid and therefore differentiation exists in this scenario. Gauri et al. (2008, p. 263) investigated the *distance to competition* as further competitor determinant on pricing strategy in retailing and found that with increasing average distance to competition, retailers rather prefer a Hi-Lo over an EDLP strategy.

2.4.2.1.4   *Manufacturer and brand factors*

As last group of determinants of pricing strategy in retailing we discuss the manufacturer and brand factors in this section. With only two papers dealing with these factors as determinants of pricing strategy in retailing, we couldn't find converging results that can be summarized. The identified results are presented in table 5 and in the following.

Hoch et al. (1994) looked at the influence of a *manufacturer's Everyday Low Purchase Price* (EDLPP) strategy on a retailer's pricing strategy. They suggested that when manufacturers pursue the EDLPP strategy, retailers should not immediately pass the prices to the consumers but instead should maintain higher margins and use "wholesale cost savings to fund more aggressive promotional activity internally, in essence a "hyper" version of Hi-Lo pricing" (p. 25). Shankar and Bolton (2004, p. 35; 38-42; 43-44) investigated the *brand preference* and the *relative brand advertising* as determinants of pricing strategy in retailing. They found that for brands with higher brand preference, retailers "charge premium prices and are less price consistent, promote more intensely, and coordinate prices and promotions more closely" (p. 43), which can be equalized with a Hi-Lo strategy (cf. Bolton/Shankar 2003, p. 220). Similarly, brands with higher relative brand advertising levels "are positively associated with premium relative brand price, price inconsistency, and price-promotion coordination" (Shankar/Bolton 2004, p. 43).

Table 5:   Empirical research on the influence of manufacturer and brand factors on pricing strategy in retailing

Author(s) Year (Journal)	Methodology	Sample (N)	Determinant(s)/ Independent Variable(s)	Dependent Variable(s)	Central Findings
Hoch et al. 1994 (JM) **R**	• Supermarket industry • Experiments ▪ Study 1: 19 categories ▪ Study 2: 26 categories ▪ Study 3: 18 categories	N=86 stores (1 retailer)	**Manufacturer factors:** • Everyday Low Purchase Price (EDLPP)	EDLP/Hi-Lo	• When a manufacturer and retailer agree on an EDLPP wholesale relationship, the retailer should not drop everyday prices at the consumer level immediately • Retailers should maintain higher margins and the wholesale cost savings to follow a "hyper" version of Hi-Lo and promote more aggressively
Shankar and Bolton 2004 (MS) **R**	• Supermarket scanner data • 6 categories • 2 years • SEM model	N=1364 brand-store combinations	**Brand factors:** • Brand preference • Relative brand advertising • (Trade deals → insufficient data)	Retailer pricing strategy (single dimensions)	• **Price consistency** is lower when brand preference and relative brand advertising are high • **Price promotion intensity** is high when brand preference is high (no significant results for relative brand advertising) • **Price promotion coordination** is higher for brands with higher brand-preference levels and relative advertising expenditures • **Relative brand price** is lower when brand preference and relative brand expenditures are lower

R = Retailer's Perspective of the Paper; JM = Journal of Marketing, MS = Marketing Science

2.4.2.2   Research on the outcomes of pricing strategy in retailing

In this chapter, the relevant empirical papers on the outcomes of pricing strategy in retailing are analyzed and discussed. We differentiated between outcomes concerning the retailer and outcomes concerning the customer and present the results for both groups separately.

2.4.2.2.1   Retailer outcomes

We found five relevant papers that examined the influence of pricing strategy on retailers. The authors examined outcomes such as sales, profitability, costs, store and chain traffic and store brand effects. As we couldn't find converging or diverging results, we aggregate the results with regard to content and present them in the following section. Table 6 gives a summary of the analyzed empirical papers on the retailer outcomes of pricing strategy in retailing. The table also shows the specific independent variables/pricing strategies and dependent variables/outcomes used in the papers.

The first identified result deals with the impact of pricing strategy on *retailer sales*. Mulhern and Leone (1990, p. 188-192) investigated "sales dollars" as an outcome of change in pricing strategy from featuring many items at small discounts, to a few items at deep discounts. This change in strategy led to an increase in chain-level sales dollars and also to an increase in store-level sales for stores located in competitive markets. For stores with only little competition from other grocery stores in their market, the change in strategy did not increase store sales and traffic. Hoch et al. (1994, p. 20) examined "sales volume" as an outcome and stated that a 10% decrease in EDLP prices led to a 3% increase in unit volume, whereas a 10% increase in Hi-Lo prices led to a 3% unit volume decrease. As the strategies mentioned in the study of Mulhern and Leone (1990) cannot be equalized with the EDLP and Hi-Lo strategy examined in the study of Hoch et al. (1994), the results of the two papers cannot really be compared and therefore no aggregation into converging or diverging results is possible.

Another outcome that was examined in connection with pricing strategy is *retailer profitability*. Hoch et al. (1994, p. 20) found that – despite the sales results shown above – a 10% increase in Hi-Lo prices led to a 15% increase in profits, whereas a 10 % decrease in EDLP prices reduced profits by 18%. In contrast, Lal and Rao (1997, p. 69) stated that industry profits are higher in an equilibrium, where retailers choose different pricing strategies (EDLP and Hi-Lo) than when stores adopt identical strategies. More specifically, in equilibrium the profits are higher for the EDLP store than for Hi-Lo store, due to the combination of pricing and communication strategy.

A further result discusses the influence of pricing strategy on *retailer costs*. Lattin and Ortmeyer (1991, p. 5) asserted that the promotional retailer benefits from lower variable or marginal costs by selling more products during trade deal periods from the manufacturer but has also additional fixed costs associated with variable pricing. The EDLP retailer benefits from reduced fixed costs (associated with variable pricing) because of lower personnel costs, fewer stocking problems and less advertising costs. Hoch et al. (1994, p. 24) stated that retailers that follow a less promotion-intense strategy will have lower costs because of warehouse and in-store efficiencies. In contrast to Lattin and Ortmeyer (1991), they didn't differentiate between variable and fixed costs.

Furthermore, the influence of pricing strategy on traffic in the store or chain is another relation examined in the study of Mulhern and Leone (1990, p. 188-192). They affirmed that a change in pricing strategy did not affect the customer traffic in the store and chain. Dhar and Hoch (1997, p. 223) investigated the influence of EDLP on store brands and asserted that in lower quality categories, the EDLP strategy benefits the store brand.

Table 6:   *Empirical research on retailer outcomes of pricing strategy in retailing*

Author(s) Year (Journal)	Methodology	Sample (N)	Independent Variable(s)	Outcome(s)/ Dependent Variable(s)	Central Findings
Dhar and Hoch 1997 (MS) R	• U.S. grocery industry • Monthly brand-level information • 34 categories, 3 years • Regression analysis	N=93 major chains	EDLP	**Retailer outcomes:** • Store brand effects	• The EDLP strategy benefits the store brand but only in lower quality categories
Hoch et al. 1994 (JM) R	• Supermarket industry • Experiments • Study 1: 19 categories • Study 2: 26 categories • Study 3: 18 categories	N=86 stores (1 retailer)	EDLP	**Retailer outcomes:** • Sales volume • Dollar profits • Costs	• A 10% EDLP category price decrease led to a 3% sales volume increase • A 10% Hi-Lo price increase led to a 3% sales decrease • An EDLP policy reduced profits by 18% • Hi-Lo pricing increased profits by 15% • Retailers pursuing less promotion-intense strategies will incur lower costs because of warehouse and in-store efficiencies
Lal and Rao 1997 (MS) R	• Supermarket industry • Game theoretic analysis	N=2 supermarkets each with 2 products	Pricing strategies (EDLP, Hi-Lo)	**Retailer outcomes:** • Profits	• In equilibrium, profits are higher for the EDLP store than for the Hi-Lo store • It is the combination of pricing and communication strategy that results in higher profits for the EDLP store
Lattin and Ortmeyer 1991 (research paper)	• Grocery industry • Game theoretic model	N=2 retailers, 1 product, 2 customer types (less	Pricing strategies (EDLP, Hi-Lo)	**Retailer outcomes:** • Costs	• The promotional retailer benefits from lower variable costs (by moving more product volume during periods of trade deal from the manufacturer) • The EDLP retailer benefits from reducing the fixed costs associated with variable pricing

Author(s) Year (Journal)	Methodology	Sample (N)	Independent Variable(s)	Outcome(s)/ Dependent Variable(s)	Central Findings
R		price sensitive, price sensitive)			
Mulhern and Leone 1990 (JBR) **R**	• Large regional grocery chain • Data on total chain and individual store sales and traffic, 2 years • Experiment; time series analysis	N not given	Change in pricing strategy from featuring many items at small discounts, to a few items at deep discounts	**Retailer outcomes:** • Total chain sales dollars • Total chain traffic • Store sales dollars • Store traffic	• The change in promotion strategy led to an increase in chain-level sales dollars but did not affect total chain traffic • The strategy change did boost sales for stores located in competitive markets, but had no impact on store traffic • The change in promotional strategy did not increase the levels of sales and traffic at the stores located in noncompetitive markets

R = Retailer's Perspective of the Paper; JBR = Journal of Business Research, JM = Journal of Marketing, MS = Marketing Science

2.4.2.2.2 Customer outcomes

Concerning the customer outcomes of pricing strategy in retailing, we found four relevant studies. Thereby outcomes such as the perception of quality, sacrifice and value, positive feelings, information processing, promotional sensitivity and brand preference were examined. Similar to the chapter on retailer outcomes, we couldn't always find converging and diverging results. Table 7 contains the analyzed papers and we summarize the findings in the following.

Suri et al. (2000, p. 199-200) as well as Suri et al. (2002, p. 166) investigated the influence of pricing strategy on the *perception of quality, value and sacrifice* of a product. As product stimulus, they used an Oxford T-Shirt. They stated that the perceived quality and value is higher when the price is presented in a fixed price format than in a discounted format. Furthermore, both studies found that the perceived sacrifice is significantly higher when the price is presented in a discounted format than as a fixed price.

Suri et al. (2002) also asserted that "subjects exposed to the fixed price format felt *significantly happier* than those exposed to the discounted price format" (p. 166) and that "the fixed price format was associated with *less uncertainty* than the discounted price format" (p. 166). Another result of their study was that the *information processing* of fixed price offers is easier than in a discount format. More detailed, they affirmed that the amount of positive and simple evaluative thoughts is higher for the fixed prices than the discounted prices, whereas the amount of negative and attribute-oriented thoughts is significantly higher for the discounted prices than the fixed prices (cf. Suri et al. 2002, p. 167).

Boatwright et al. (2004, p. 179-185) investigated *"promotional sensitivity"* as an outcome of pricing strategy in retailing. Thereby price response, display and feature response, response to competing account price and response to competing brand price were investigated as factors of promotional sensitivity. They found that EDLP customers are less price sensitive than Hi-Lo customers. Furthermore, they stated that EDLP accounts are less responsive to displays and features and that EDLP consumers are less sensitive to competing brands than Hi-Lo customers. In general they asserted that in high competitive markets, there is a greater sensitivity to competing account price.

Pechtl (2004, p. 229) found that EDLP prone consumers have a stronger *preference for well-known brands* than Hi-Lo prone consumers.

Table 7:   Empirical research on customer outcomes of pricing strategy in retailing

Author(s) Year (Journal)	Methodology	Sample (N)	Independent Variable(s)	Outcome(s)/ Dependent Variable(s)	Central Findings
Boatwright et al. 2004 (QME) C	• Account level (=market-retailer combination) data • 120 weeks • Ground coffee product, 2 major national brands • Bayesian Hierachical model	N=97 US retail accounts	Account retail strategy (EDLP or Hi-Lo)	**Customer outcomes:** Promotional sensitivity (price response, display and feature response, response to competing account price, response to competing brand price)	• Consumers who shop at EDLP stores are less sensitive to short term price changes than consumers at non-EDLP/Hi-Lo stores • Consumers at EDLP stores can be assured of lower average prices and do not have as much incentive to track deals and switch stores as consumers in Hi-Lo stores • EDLP accounts are much less responsive to displays and features • In market areas with greater competition there is greater sensitivity to competing account price • EDLP customers are less sensitive to competing brand prices
Pechtl 2004 (JRCS) C	• Interviews in 2 large grocery stores in Germany (2000) • Cluster Analysis, T-Test, ANOVA	N=620 shoppers	Store choice (EDLP or Hi-Lo)	**Customer outcomes:** • Brand preference	• EDLP prone consumers exhibit a stronger preference for well-known brands than Hi-Lo prone consumers
Suri et al. 2000 (JPBM) C	• Experiment with Oxford shirt as product stimulus • MANOVA	N=44 students	Fixed format vs. discount format	**Customer outcomes:** • Perception of quality • Perception of sacrifice • Perception of	• The perception of quality is higher when price information is presented in a fixed price format than in a discount format • The perception of sacrifice is higher when price information is presented in a discount format than in a fixed price format • The perception of value is higher when price

Author(s) Year (Journal)	Methodology	Sample (N)	Independent Variable(s)	Outcome(s)/ Dependent Variable(s)	Central Findings
				value	information is presented in a fixed price format than in a discount format
Suri et al. 2002 (JPBM) C	• Experiment with Oxford shirt as product stimulus • MANOVA	N=34 students	Fixed format vs. discount format	**Customer outcomes:** • Positive effect • Information processing • Perception of quality • Perception of sacrifice • Perception of value	• The evaluation of fixed price offers is associated with stronger positive effect (happier, less uncertain) • The evaluation of fixed price offers is associated with less thorough processing of price information than in a discount format • Perceptions of quality and value are significantly higher when price information is presented in a fixed price format than in a discount format • Perceptions of quality is significantly higher when the price is presented as a discounted price than as a fixed price

C = Customer's Perspective of the Paper; JPBM = Journal of Product and Brand Management, JRCS = Journal of Retailing and Consumer Services, QME = Quantitative Marketing and Economics

2.5 Implications

Until now there has not been much research on pricing strategy in retailing. Based on our literature review, we derive and prioritize directions for future research as well as implications for managerial action in the following.

2.5.1 Directions for future research

1. Detailed measurement of pricing strategy in retailing: as the review of the definitions shows, most researchers define pricing strategy in retailing as a bivariate variable with two possibilities Hi-Lo and EDLP. A more detailed measurement of pricing strategy in retailing would be adequate, taking into account the complex circumstances under which retailers act, reflected by complex assortments with many different products and prices. It could be interesting to build an index representing the extent of the pursuit of pricing strategy as a continuum. Furthermore and as an extension of the work of Bolton/Shankar (2003), a typology of different pricing strategies at the store level could be developed. In this context it would be interesting to work with objective scanner data with different product categories from different types of retailers.

2. Retailer-related outcomes of pricing strategy in retailing: most of the existing papers have examined the determinants of pricing strategy in retailing. Future research should therefore focus on the outcomes of pricing strategy in retailing. Retailer-related outcomes like sales, turnover, profitability, costs, in-store traffic and average receipt amount of the pricing strategy could be investigated, as this field has been largely neglected in the existing research. One could compare short-term and long-term profitability of different pricing strategies with a survey. Another possibility would be to work with objective data from different stores e.g. with information on sales and turnover.

3. Customer-related outcomes of pricing strategy in retailing: besides the retailer-related outcomes, also more research could be done on customer-related outcomes. Future research could examine promotional sensitivity, brand preference, customer's mood and information processing as outcomes and check if the results are convergent or divergent to the existing research of Boatwright et al. (2004), Pechtl (2004) and Suri et al. (2000, 2002). Furthermore, the study of Suri et al. (2000 and 2002) with perception of quality, value and sacrifice as outcomes could be replicated with a bigger non-student sample and within the grocery sector. Further interesting customer-related outcomes are customer loyalty, cross-and up-selling potential and price image.

4. Influence of pricing strategy on price image: especially the impact of pricing strategies on the perceived price image of a retailer would be a very interesting field for future research. The topic of price image was heavily investigated as an outcome of price promotions (e.g. cf. Nyström et al. 1975) but not with regard to pricing strategies.

5. Influence of competitor factors on pricing strategy in retailing: in the existing literature, competitor factors build the most important determinant of pricing strategy in retailing. Despite this fact, there is not much research on this topic. Especially the distance to competition is an interesting factor as only the paper of Gauri et al. (2008) considered this until now. Another interesting determinant could be the number of competitors nearby, which was not included in any of the analyzed papers.

6. Influence of retailer factors on pricing strategy in retailing: as seen in the literature review (table 2), many studies investigated market and consumer factors as determinants of pricing strategy in retailing. Much less research was conducted concerning the influence of retailer factors on pricing strategy in retailing. Within the subgroup "assortment and category factors", aspects such as category type (storable, necessary), assortment size (smaller vs. larger), assortment heterogeneity and assortment perishability could be investigated. Within the subgroup "store factors" one could build on the research of Ellickson/Misra (2008) and Gauri et al. (2008) and examine the influence of vertically integrated stores or the number of services in a store on pricing strategy in retailing. Furthermore, costs play an important role in formulating a pricing strategy (cf. Nagle et al. 2011, p. 197), so it would be interesting to investigate how costs may influence the pricing strategy of a retailer.

7. Influence of manufacturer and brand factors on pricing strategy in retailing: it would be interesting to extend the study of Hoch et al. (1994) who focused on the manufacturer's EDLPP as a determinant of the retailer's pricing strategy. Other manufacturers' pricing strategies could be used as determinants. Besides that, the extent of brand advertising could be examined, building on the study of Shankar/Bolton (2004). The brand strength could also be an interesting determinant. At the store level one could question if retailers differ in their pricing strategy with regard to the rate of strong brands in their assortment.

8. Research from the retailer's point of view: despite the fact that pricing strategy is an important concern of the company, many researchers regard this topic from the customer's point of view. It would be desirable if more studies would consider the retailer's perspective, e.g. through interviews or experiments in the retailing industry.

9. Research from the pricing strategy perspective: there are many studies that investigated the determinants and outcomes of the tactical instrument of price promotions. More studies from the perspective of pricing strategy would be desirable. In today's retailing practice, pricing strategy is still seen as a rather short-term day-to-day decision. It may be a fruitful area to do more detailed research on the determinants and outcomes of long-term store level pricing strategies in retailing. Thereby research could create more awareness of this important topic in the retailing practice and could derive interesting managerial implications for retailers.

10. Pricing strategy at the category level: though the pricing strategy in retailing is defined at the store level, it would be interesting to examine different categories with regard to the pursued pricing strategy and compare the results. Thereby it would be also desirable to work with objective scanner data containing a representative selection of different product categories in a "product basket".

11. Influence of further determinants: it would be a fruitful avenue for future research to examine further factors influencing the choice of pricing strategy in retailing such as regulations by law. Until now, no empirical investigation has considered this aspect. Furthermore, pricing history (cf. Nijs et al. 2007) could be another interesting direction of future research.

12. Online vs. offline pricing strategies: It would be a very fruitful area to investigate if retailers pursue different pricing strategies or extents of pricing strategies in their offline and online channels. Is there a higher extent of Hi-Lo pricing strategy online vs. offline? Or are there totally different types of pricing strategies in the online world? Do other factors than identified for offline retailers determine the online pricing strategy? How do online pricing strategies affect consumer online and offline shopping behavior? In this context, it could be interesting to examine data from a grocery retailer that started to operate online.

2.5.2 Managerial implications

1. Definition of the pricing strategy in retailing: Our literature review showed that there exists no consistent definition of the term pricing strategy in retailing. For retail firms it is even more important to define a clear pricing strategy in order to create a clear positioning for the customers. Retailers should therefore clearly define if they rather pursue an EDLP or a Hi-Lo pricing strategy and if they determine the pricing strategy at the product-, assortment- or store-level. Furthermore, retailers should view the pricing strategy more like a positioning strategy, including elements like service and communication decisions.

2. *Change of pricing strategy:* Retailers should be aware of possible consequences when switching their pricing strategy, e.g. from Hi-Lo to EDLP. A change towards EDLP could on the one hand lead to smoother demand, fewer residuals, more efficient inventory management, more efficient use of personnel, more advertising flexibility and more consumer appeal but on the other hand could also involve the risk of confusing customers, whose pricing perceptions have been conditioned by past pricing practices and of erupting price wars which could lead to a substantial decline in retailer profits (cf. Ortmeyer et al. 1991).

3. *Influence of market and consumer factors on pricing strategy in retailing:* In general, retail managers can use the converging results to determine in which areas (income, population) to build or buy new stores, which customer segments (time-constrained service/price seekers, cherry pickers) to focus on, how to take into account the price sensitivity, the shopping frequency or the size of the shopping basket of customers etc. Specifically, one of the converging results indicated that consumers with lower income prefer EDLP, whereas consumers with higher income prefer Hi-Lo. Therefore EDLP/Hi-Lo retailers should position themselves rather in lower/higher income areas. Furthermore, EDLP/Hi-Lo retailers should think about how to attract the higher/lower income segment.

4. *Influence of competitor factors on pricing strategy in retailing:* Our literature analysis showed that retailers match their own pricing strategy with their competitor's pricing strategy. According to this result, retailers don't differentiate with regard to pricing strategy. With many retailers having similar pricing strategies in one area, price wars can easily erupt and thus retailer profits will probably diminish drastically. Therefore, retail managers should rethink their competitor-driven choice of pricing strategy. They could rather use factors such as service or assortment to differentiate themselves from their competitors and attract customers.

5. *Retailer outcomes of pricing strategy in retailing:* Within the retailer outcomes, we couldn't find converging results. Existing research therefore cannot give clear advice, which pricing strategy is better in terms of sales dollars, sales volume, costs, store traffic or profitability. Lal/Rao (1997) stated that industry profits are higher when retailers choose different pricing strategies, than when stores adopt identical strategies. This supports our argumentation in the previous point.

6. *Customer outcomes of pricing strategy in retailing:* Similar to the retailer outcomes, also for the customer outcomes, no converging results could be found. Nevertheless, there are interesting results for retail managers. The finding of Boatwright et al. (2004), that EDLP customers are less price sensitive than

Hi-Lo customers shows, that through the use of more and more price promotions, customers are educated to become more price sensitive. Retailers should be careful when implementing price promotions and reductions because this could lead to price wars and thus to a decrease in profits for the whole retail industry.

2.6 Conclusion

This paper gives an overview of the state-of-the-art of research on the topic of pricing strategy in retailing. Based on the description of the theoretical foundations, different definitions of pricing strategy in retailing are analyzed and discussed in detail. Then a comprehensive review of the relevant conceptual and empirical articles is given. Thereby we first classified the relevant research into conceptual and empirical studies. For the empirical papers, a further allocation of studies about determinants and outcomes of pricing strategy in retailing is carried out. The results of both the conceptual and empirical studies are discussed while presenting main as well as further results.

The analysis of the determinants shows that many papers examined the influence of market and consumer factors, retailer factors, competitor factors and manufacturer and brand factors on pricing strategy in retailing. Thereby research mainly addresses the influence of market and consumer factors on pricing strategy in retailing and finds converging results concerning income, family size, size of the shopping basket, population density, shopping frequency, time-constrained consumers vs. cherry pickers, price sensitivity, sale proneness, store loyalty and fixed and variable costs and utiliy. Among the retailer determinants, converging results concerning the influence of store and chain size on pricing strategy are found. Among the competitor determinants, the only but most important converging result found is the influence of competitor pricing strategy on the retailer's pricing strategy. Regarding the manufacturer and brand factors as determinants, no converging results were found.

The investigated outcomes of pricing strategy in retailing were grouped into retailer and customer outcomes. We found five studies concerning the retailer outcomes and four studies concerning the customer outcomes of pricing strategy. No converging results for both types of outcomes could be asserted. On the basis of the analyzed literature, fruitful avenues for future research as well as implications for managerial action were presented and prioritized. Thereby it became clear that the topic of pricing strategy in retailing contains many unanswered research questions: how can pricing strategies in retailing be adequately measured in order to represent the complex circumstances in retailing? How does pricing strategy influence customer- and retailer-related outcome variables? What influence on price image do certain pricing strategies have? Do certain pricing strategies differ in terms of short-term vs. long-term profitability? What are important determinants of pricing strategy in retailing? Do retailers that operate in multiple channels pursue different pricing strategies in the different channels? Future research can try to give answers to these and many other interesting research questions.

In the following chapters, we will try to give answers to some of these research questions: chapter 3 contains an empirical analysis of pricing strategy in retailing at the store level, its outcomes and moderating effects. In chapter 4 we investigate pricing strategies in retailing and their impact on sales dollars per squaremeter at the category level. Besides the theory, our review also presents several implications for managerial action. Retail firms should define a clear pricing strategy in order to create a clear positioning for the customer. Furthermore, retailers should be aware of the chances and risks connected with a change in pricing strategy. Moreover, retail managers can use the results to determine, how to take into account certain determinants and outcomes of pricing strategy in retailing.

3 Don't get Stuck in the Middle! An Examination of Pure versus Hybrid Pricing Strategies in Retailing[2]

3.1 Introduction

In chapter 2 we explained the importance of pricing strategy in retailing and provided a comprehensive literature review about this topic. We build on our theoretical basis from chapter two and design a study about the impact of an EDLP versus Hi-Lo pricing strategy on financial outcomes. We address some of the directions for future research, named in chapter 2 in this study: for example we provide a detailed measurement of pricing strategy in retailing, we include retailer related outcomes in our model such as sales dollars per squaremeter and sales volume per squaremeter and we look at the influence of competitor factors and retailer factors on the relation between pricing strategy in retailing and the retailer related outcomes. It was also addressed to conduct more research from the pricing strategy perspective, as there are many studies about pricing tactics and price promotions. In general, this study is an empirical examination of pricing strategies from the retailer's point of view, as also named as a fruitful future research direction in chapter 2.

The following study is based on the unpublished manuscript of Fassnacht, El Husseini and DeKinder 2012.

As also stated in chapter two, in practice, retailers typically want to accomplish a *multitude of objectives* with their pricing strategy (Bailey 2008; Hoch, Dreze, and Purk 1994). As a result, many retailers end up pursuing a "hybrid" pricing strategy, incorporating elements of both EDLP and Hi-Lo. This highlights that while most characterizations of retail pricing strategies suggest that retailers use *either* an EDLP or a Hi-Lo strategy (cf. Bailey 2008; Cataluna, Franco, and Ramos 2005; Kopalle et al. 2009; Lal and Rao 1997; Lattin and Ortmeyer 1991; Monroe 2003; Pechtl 2004), a closer look at retailer behavior reveals that many retailers may actually pursue a bit of *both* pricing strategies.

Although many retailers are pursuing a hybrid strategy, it is unclear how well these hybrid strategies work. In many cases managers are pursuing hybrid pricing strategies in order to appeal to a greater amount of consumers, while balancing firm and market-level issues. However, research has not investigated whether this hybrid approach pays off in terms of overall retail performance. Prior research based on Porter's (1980) generic competitive strategies

---

2   Based on an unpublished manuscript of Fassnacht/El Husseini/DeKinder (2012)

framework suggests that firms are more successful if they focus on one strategy rather than following hybrid strategies (cf. Allen et al. 2007; Kim, Nam, and Stimpert 2004; Shah 2007; Thornhill and White 2007; Wright et al. 1990). However, there is also considerable research that criticizes this view and finds that following a hybrid strategy is more successful than focusing on one strategy (cf. Hill 1988; Miller and Friesen 1986; Murray 1988; Pertusa-Ortega, Molina-Azoin and Claver-Cortez 2009; Pervaiz and Rafiq 1992; Wright et al. 1990). Until now, these two opposing views have not been examined in the context of retail pricing strategies. In this research we build on prior work by investigating the following research question: is it better to focus on either a strong Hi-Lo or EDLP strategy, or use a hybrid pricing strategy somewhere in the middle?

Despite the importance of understanding the performance outcomes of a retailer's pricing strategy, our research question has not been answered by the marketing literature. Specifically, our research is distinct from prior research in three important ways. First, there has been extensive investigation on pricing *tactics* and especially price promotions, but a comprehensive examination of pricing *strategies* is still missing, as postulated by other researchers (Voss and Seiders 2003). Second, Gauri, Trivedi, and Grewal (2008, p. 256) note that considerable research centers on how pricing strategies affect *consumer behavior* such as store choice and response to strategies based on consumer profiles. However, far less attention has been focused on the effectiveness of these pricing strategies from *the retailer's perspective*, i.e., examining retailer performance outcomes. Finally, the few studies on retailer pricing strategies offer insight at the brand-store level (Bolton and Shankar 2003; Gauri, Trivedi and Grewal 2008) rather than at the store level. Store level insights are an important addition to existing research. We conducted a qualitative pre-study with eleven expert interviews from the consumer goods, retailing, consulting and market research industries and found that managers want information about the effectiveness of pricing strategies at the *store level*. They indicated that store level analyses are important because it influences their decisions regarding training, policy making, and incentive structures. As one Managing Director of an international market research and consulting company noted, "The basic decision about a pricing strategy – Hi-Lo or EDLP – has to be understood at the store level."

Our research aims to build on existing research to generate a better understanding of retail pricing strategies. In doing so, we make two major contributions to the literature. First, we conceptualize a construct that captures a store-level retail pricing strategy. To develop this construct we build on both our qualitative interviews and existing research. Our interviews with active managers suggest that the trade-offs between EDLP and Hi-Lo Pricing is of significant interest for retail managers. In fact, most managers we interviewed feel that a classically defined Hi-Lo and EDLP pricing strategy doesn't exist anymore and that in practice pricing strategies are much more complex, including decisions about price promotions, displays and features. To capture this complexity of pricing strategies in retailing, we create our focal construct "Pricing Strategy Alignment", reflecting a continuum with Hi-Lo and EDLP at the extremes and hybrid strategies in between. Despite calls in previous research to create a comprehensive measure for pricing strategies (Voss and Seiders 2003), to our knowledge, such a measure has not been created before.

Second, this study is the first to answer the question: how does a hybrid pricing strategy affect retailer performance. Many studies have investigated the factors that affect a retailer's decision to pursue a particular pricing strategy (i.e., antecedents to pricing strategy), however the theoretical and empirical link between store-level pricing strategy and store performance is not investigated to date (Bolton and Shankar 2003; Gauri, Trivedi, and Grewal 2008). One challenge for such an investigation has been the availability of objective retailer performance data. However, our data from 931 retail stores over a two-year period allows us to empirically test the effectiveness of pricing strategy alignment on two important measures in retailing: sales dollars per sqm (Mulhern and Leone 1990) and sales volume per sqm (Hoch, Dreze, and Purk 1994). We hypothesize and find support for a non-linear relationship between our focal construct "pricing strategy alignment" and the outcome variables, indicating that retailers are better off aligning their behaviors with one strategy rather than moving to the middle and creating a hybrid pricing strategy. In addition, we test for moderating effects of store, market and competitive characteristics on the relationship between pricing strategy alignment and retailer sales performance and find that hybrid strategies can be particularly ineffective in certain situations (Ingene and Brown 1987).

The remainder of the paper is organized as follows: we will introduce our conceptual framework and discuss the outcomes of pricing strategy alignment as well as possible moderator effects. Then, we describe the sample, data collection, measurement of the variables and show the empirical results of the analyses. We conclude by discussing the implications of our findings for researchers and managers and outlining the limitations and ideas for future research.

3.2   Conceptual framework and hypotheses

The goal of our research is to address the unanswered question of whether or not hybrid, versus clearly aligned EDLP or Hi-Lo, pricing strategies are effective for retailers. To achieve this goal we had to accomplish the following: (i) develop a measure that captures retailer hybrid pricing strategies; (ii) measure and test for the effects of a hybrid pricing strategy on firm performance; and (iii) identify and examine variables that may moderate the relationship between a hybrid pricing strategy and firm performance. These tasks are the basis of our

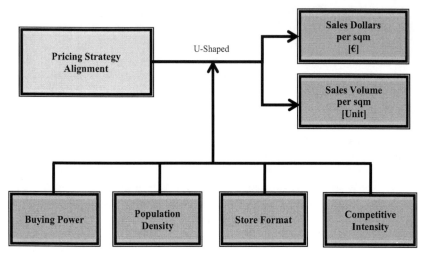

conceptual model, shown in figure 3. Our conceptual model was developed using both extensive qualitative research we conducted for this specific project and existing literature.

Figure 3:   Conceptual framework for empirical analyses

3.2.1   Qualitative pre-study

To develop our focal construct, i.e., pricing strategy alignment, as well as our holistic conceptual model, we conducted a qualitative pre-study. We recruited managers from different industries, with different functions and hierarchical levels (cf. Bendapudi and Leone 2002; Kohli and Jaworski 1990; Menon et al. 1999; Tuli, Kohli, and Bharadwaj 2007). To recruit the participants, we mostly used personal contacts; however we also utilized cold calls to recruit potential participants. In total, we conducted 11 expert interviews with CEOs and high-ranked managers from the following industries: retailing, consumer goods, consulting and marketing research. Before each interview, we prepared and sent a powerpoint-presentation containing detailed information about the research topic and the current status of the project. This step provided important information at the outset of our research investigation because potential participants responded very eagerly based on the topic alone. In fact, the CEO of a top retailer responded and noted that "I usually do not use my own time for meetings like this, however the topic of EDLP versus Hi-Lo pricing is of such importance to our organization that I would like to speak with you and participate in this research[3]". This sentiment was expressed on some level by every one of our managerial participants.

The interviews lasted between 20 and 60 minutes and were conducted in person or by phone. We used a structured set of questions for the expert interviews (see Appendix). These questions were used as a general framework, but further questions were added during the interview in order to gain more clarification, concrete examples and greater detail regarding interesting responses. The interviews were not recorded because of the sensitivity of the subject of pricing strategies. Therefore, the authors took special consideration to take detailed notes during the interviews in order to create transcripts after each interview.

There were several important insights gleaned from the qualitative pre-study. First, managers had significant interest in the answer to our research question. Managers noted that "pricing is incredibly complex" and that many of them were "currently wrestling with the trade-offs of EDLP versus Hi-Lo pricing". As one manager noted, "I believe your focus on the trade-off between Hi-Lo and EDLP is very interesting, and there is not much information available to managers on that topic right now". Second, managers indicated that in their positions of leadership, they had the important task of setting the strategic direction for their retail stores, including training employees, determining incentive structures, and allocating pivotal resources. Many of the managers indicated that their chosen pricing strategy had implications for all of these other decisions. As such, they wanted a better understanding of how store-level pricing strategies affect performance outcomes. Finally, managers stated that they viewed pricing strategies on a continuum where many retailers use some

---

3   The majority of our interviews were conducted in the German language. All of the quotes placed in direct quotation marks are, in fact, translated versions of the German quotes. Each quote was translated to the best of the authors' ability and then checked by an additional bi-lingual researcher for accuracy.

aspects of EDLP as well as other aspects from Hi-Lo. In fact, many of the managers indicated that their own retail stores were somewhere along the continuum rather than aligned with one strategy or the other.

These insights guided us on two important components of how to measure our focal construct. First, while some research suggests that pricing strategy may not be best measured on a continuum (Bolton and Shankar 2003), our findings from the qualitative study were consistent with other research that does measure pricing strategy on a continuum (Hoch, Dreze, and Purk 1994; Shankar and Bolton 2004). Second, our extensive interviews suggested that our measure should be at the store level. The main motivation for managers wanting a store-level measure was to understand holistic implications for individual decisions. The managers revealed that within a given store it was common to find that pricing strategies differ by product category. For example, one category manager may decide that for his/her particular category a Hi-Lo-oriented pricing strategy is the most effective way to optimize performance. *Within the same store*, however, a different category manager may decide that an EDLP-oriented pricing strategy is the most effective way to optimize performance in his/her particular product category. As a result, *within the same store there are different approaches being used in different product categories*. While each approach may be optimal at the category level, the managers we interviewed indicated it was important for them to understand what effect this has when it ultimately results in a hybrid pricing strategy at the store level. As such, based on our qualitative pre-study, we contribute to the existing literature by conceptualizing and investigating pricing strategy alignment at the store level.

3.2.2 Developing the focal construct: comparing literature and field perspectives

EDLP, Hi-Lo, and Hybrid Pricing Strategies. A review of existing literature reveals that there are different definitions of pricing strategy in retailing. Most of the definitions include two store-wide pricing strategies – the Hi-Lo or the EDLP pricing strategy – and regard pricing strategy as a dichotomous variable (Bailey 2008; Cataluna, Franco, and Ramos 2005; Kopalle et al. 2009; Lal and Rao 1997; Lattin and Ortmeyer 1991; Monroe 2003; Pechtl 2004). A Hi-Lo strategy involves higher regular prices with steep temporary discounts whereas an EDLP strategy is characterized by consistently low prices (cf. Bolton, Shankar, and Montoya 2010). But many authors see Hi-Lo and EDLP not just as two options of a bipolar classification scheme, but rather as the poles of a continuum with hybrid strategies in between (Bell and Lattin 1998; Ellickson and Misra 2008; Hoch, Dreze, and Purk 1994; Popkowski Leszczyc, Sinha, and Saghal 2004; Tang, Bell, and Ho 2001). For example, in the German retail market, Rewe is seen as a Hi-Lo retailer, but Rewe also has EDLP elements with its private label brands. In addition, other examples include Aldi and dm which are retailers that pursue EDLP strategies, but will also offer some products on promotion. These examples of focusing on one strategy, yet using components of the other strategy are what we term "hybrid" pricing strategies. In the U.S. retail market, Wal Mart follows an EDLP strategy for most of its stores (73%), but also follows a hybrid strategy in 26% of the stores. Another example is the retailer Pathmark, which follows different pricing strategies in its stores: 42% follow a Hi-Lo strategy, 33% follow an EDLP strategy and the remaining 25% follow a hybrid strategy (Ellickson and Misra 2008).

Pricing Strategy as a Multi-Dimensional Construct. The term "pricing strategy" has been used differently where in some cases it is a one-dimensional construct and in other cases it is a multi-dimensional construct. Research that defines it using one single dimension tends to focus on price variation when defining and measuring pricing strategy (cf. Bell and Lattin 1998; Ellickson and Misra 2008; Hoch, Dreze, and Purk 1994; Lattin and Ortmeyer 1991; Ortmeyer et al. 1991; Pechtl 2004; Tang et al. 2001). In contrast, there are authors that regard pricing strategy in retailing as a multi-dimensional construct which contains not only measures price variation, but also promotion and communication measures associated with pricing (cf. Bolton and Shankar 2003; Neslin, Shoemaker, and Krishna 1994; Shankar and Bolton 2004; Shankar and Krishnamurthi 1996; Voss and Seiders 2003). These multi-dimensional approaches are adopted because of a belief that the pure price focus is not comprehensive enough to mirror the strategic character of a pricing strategy. Moreover, it reflects the idea that a pricing strategy encompasses not only how a firm prices its products, but also how those prices are discounted over time, the depth of price discounts, the frequency of price discounts, and the communication of price discounts to consumers.

In this research we conceptualize pricing strategy using the multi-dimensional approach (Bolton and Shankar 2003; Neslin, Shoemaker, and Krishna 1994; Shankar and Bolton 2004; Shankar and Krishnamurthi 1996; Voss and Seiders 2003). We argue that a comprehensive measure is important in order to distinguish a *pricing strategy* from an individual *pricing tactic*. Furthermore, we believe that these multiple dimensions work together and represent an overall strategic force that guides decisions (cf. Bolton and Shankar 2003; Voss and Seiders 2003). A comprehensive measurement takes into account that retailers act under complex circumstances and have to make *several* different decisions which all reflect an overarching pricing strategy.

Our measure consists of three dimensions:
  (1) price variation,
  (2) deal intensity and
  (3) deal support (Shankar and Bolton 2004).

Each of these dimensions will differ for an EDLP versus Hi-Lo pricing strategy. *Price variation* captures the consistency of prices over time. For an EDLP pricing strategy there is a low level of price variation because prices are priced low to begin with, and are infrequently discounted. On the other hand, with a Hi-Lo pricing strategy price variation is high because of the frequent and steep discounts. *Deal intensity* captures the frequency and depth with which the retailer offers deals. Deals pertain strictly to price reductions, and do not include other promotional incentives such as extra volume. The score for deal intensity will be increased with: (i) greater frequency of offering deals; (ii) greater depth in the discounts; and (iii) greater duration of the deals. Again, the score for deal intensity is low in the case of an EDLP pricing strategy, but high for a Hi-Lo pricing strategy. Finally, *deal support* captures the coordination between the pricing deal and the displays and/or features within the store to promote the price discount. Again, the score for deal support is low in the case of an EDLP pricing strategy, but high for a Hi-Lo pricing strategy (Bolton and Shankar 2003; Hoch, Dreze, and Purk 1994; Voss and Seiders 2003).

   The main contribution of this research is to investigate the effects of a hybrid pricing strategy on retailer sales performance. To measure a hybrid pricing strategy we aggregate all three dimensions (price variation, deal intensity and deal support) across all product categories for a given store. A hybrid strategy will result in a moderate score of this aggregated measure. This moderate score is a result of one of two scenarios: (i) within a store, different product categories are using the two different pricing strategies (EDLP and Hi-Lo) and therefore when aggregated at the store level the overall store pricing strategy is a hybrid pricing strategy; or (ii) within a store, the marketing managers have adopted a moderate level of pricing variation, deal intensity and deal support, i.e., they are using some of the Hi-Lo pricing strategy tactics but doing so at a more moderate level than their competitors. In sum, very low scores for price variation, deal intensity and deal support indicate that the store pricing strategy is very aligned with an EDLP pricing strategy; very high scores for price variation, deal intensity and deal support indicate that the pricing strategy is very aligned with a Hi-Lo pricing strategy; and moderate scores for price variation, deal intensity and deal support indicate that the pricing strategy is not aligned and the store has adopted a hybrid pricing strategy.

3.2.3 The effects of pricing strategy alignement

Porter (1980) argues that firms which fail to follow one of the three generic strategies "cost leadership", "differentiation" and "focus" are essentially "stuck in the middle" (Porter 1980, p. 41). Firms that are stuck in the middle pursuing hybrid strategies have an inferior strategic position in the competitive market with "almost guaranteed low profitability" (Porter 1980, p. 41). A stuck in the middle position derives from "a blurred corporate culture and a conflicting set of organizational arrangements and motivation system" (Porter 1980, p. 42) and therefore from the inability or unwillingness of the firm to make clear strategic decisions.

While Porter's original work (and subsequent supporting research) suggests that hybrid strategies will result in poor performance, there is also considerable research that criticizes this view and finds that following a hybrid strategy is more successful than focusing on one strategy (cf. Hill 1988; Miller and Friesen 1986; Murray 1988; Pertusa-Ortega, Molina-Azoin and Claver-Cortez 2009; Pervaiz and Rafiq 1992; Wright et al. 1990). According to these researchers, there are several problems connected with pure strategies. First, the pursuit of a pure versus a hybrid strategy may lead to weaknesses in product offerings because of ignoring certain customer needs. Second, pure strategies may be more easily imitated by competitors than hybrid strategies. Third, firms following pure strategies may be more vulnerable regarding market changes and changing customer needs. In sum, hybrid strategies may fulfill customer needs more precisely, may be more difficult to copy and may provide a more flexible environment to respond and make strategic changes.

We reconcile these two views by invoking three specific consequences of a hybrid pricing strategy in the grocery retail setting. First, a hybrid pricing strategy affects a firm's ability to use other marketing tactics consistently and effectively. Within a retail environment there are several decision-makers who are using many different marketing tactics including price discounts and the support of those discounts through displays and/or features. In general, hybrid strategies are complex which makes it difficult to set priorities. They cause confusion and a loss of direction for managers within the store. More specifically, it makes it difficult to build synergies within a store. And, synergies are helpful in creating greater performance. More specifically, it is noted that "Synergies may also arise from intangible resource commonalities that result in an ability to share management expertise or know-how across several related business segments" (p. 1028, Harrison, Hall, and Nargundkar 1993). A lack of coordinated marketing effort is likely to make each individual price-promotion less effective because of losing out on additional know-how and expertise from all of the managers in a given store. Furthermore, Harrison, Hall, and Nargundkar (1993) also note that a lack of synergies makes "skill transference and proper management difficult", and "make physical resource sharing" very difficult which reduces "the probability of identifying and exploiting synergies based on existing tangible resource commonalities" (p. 1032). As such, stores that are less synergistic with their pricing efforts (i.e., follow a hybrid pricing strategy) will have less effective marketing efforts and therefore will generate less volume and dollar sales than a store with an aligned and synergistic pricing strategy.

Second, a store that pursues a hybrid pricing strategy is likely to experience the "downsides" of each pricing strategy, without the "upsides" to offset them. More specifically, for an EDLP pricing strategy to work effectively the store has to maintain low costs (i.e., by not spending money on discounts or promotions of such discounts). However, a store that has low prices, but still offers discounts must pay for the deals without the revenue of the "everyday high prices" to offset it. Furthermore, those stores will attract the known "cherry pickers" without the benefit of the less price sensitive consumer paying the high regular price that Hi-Lo pricing strategies use to offset the discounted prices. As such, when pursuing both strategies a store may maintain the sales volume but we anticipate that the store will make itself vulnerable to lower sales dollars than a store using EDLP or Hi-Lo because of not having the benefits of an aligned strategy to offset the costs.

Finally, pricing has significant impact on consumer decision making. Extensive research indicates that consumers use prices as indicators of quality and/or value (Rao 2005; Shiv, Carmon, and Ariely 2005; Brown 1969). When making store choices a consumer takes many factors into consideration, and one key consideration is the price they anticipate finding at the store (Briesch, Chintagunta and Fox 2009). A consumer's expectations about price will be based on past experience as well as the retailer's pricing strategy which is "designed to communicate a price position to consumers," (p. 37, Voss and Seiders 2003). As a result, inconsistent pricing and/or inconsistent messaging within a store can have implications for consumer perceptions. We argue that a lack of consistent pricing and messaging across product categories within a store is likely to result in consumers having uncertainty about what prices to expect from that store. For example, if a consumer is purchasing laundry detergent form the store and observes that the prices of all the detergents are lower than competitors then the consumer will assume the store uses an EDLP strategy. If that same consumer then goes to buy yogurt and finds much higher prices for all of the products, then the consumer will update their impression about EDLP and may decide to wait until there is a price promotion to buy the yogurt he/she wants. If this same consumer then wants to buy something from a product category with which he/she is not familiar with the pricing or has no prior experience (e.g. birthday candles), he/she will hesitate because he/she does not have confidence in how competitive the store's prices are. Having an unclear view of what the pricing strategy is will cause uncertainty about the value of a purchase and lead consumer to question whether they are getting "a deal" or being "ripped off" in unfamiliar product categories. This uncertainty about prices and overall value will result in consumers preferring other stores and therefore decrease their likelihood to patron a retailer with inconsistent pricing in the store. Ultimately this will generate less volume and dollar sales per sqm for stores that choose hybrid pricing strategies, relative to stores that align with either an EDLP or Hi-Lo pricing strategy.

Based on the three reasons argued above, we propose that retailers are likely to achieve greater sales performance by pursuing an EDLP or Hi-Lo pricing strategy rather than a hybrid strategy. As such, pricing strategy alignment should have a U-shaped relationship with performance such that aligning with either pricing strategy on the ends of the continuum is better than pursuing a hybrid strategy in the middle. More formally we hypothesize:

H1: There is a U-shaped relationship between a retailer's pricing strategy alignment and the sales dollars per sqm for the retailer.

H2: There is a U-shaped relationship between a retailer's pricing strategy alignment and the sales volume per sqm for the retailer.

3.2.4 Moderating effects

Contingency theory stresses the important influence of situational factors on how an organization is managed and questions the existence of one optimal way to manage or organize (Zeithaml, Varadarajan, and Zeithaml 1988). Following this theory, it is important to identify situational factors that may influence the effectiveness of a particular business strategy. This is likely to be the case with a retailer's pricing strategy. According to Gauri, Trivedi, and Grewal (2008) and Ingene and Brown (1987), there are three general categories of factors that affect retailer strategy: market, store and competitive characteristics. Using this framework, we investigate how market, store and competitive characteristics moderate the relationship between pricing strategy alignment and retailer sales performance (see Figure 1).

3.2.4.1 Market factors

Buying power and population density have been identified as two important market factors that impact retailer pricing strategy. *Buying power* refers to the level of income of a retailer's potential customers and has been shown to have direct and moderating effects on pricing strategy in retailing (Bailey 2008; Bell, Ho, and Tang 1998; Ellickson and Misra 2008; Popkowski Leszczyc, Sinha, and Saghal 2004; Popkowski Leszczyc, Sinha, and Timmermans 2000). *Population density* refers to the concentration of potential customers in a retailer's geographic area and is acknowledged as a likely situational factor affecting pricing strategy in retailing (Shankar and Bolton 2004).

Buying power. To optimize the effectiveness of a pricing strategy, retailers should take into consideration the appeal of a given pricing strategy to its potential consumers (Ellickson and Misra 2008). Of particular relevance is how consumer income affects the appeal of a pricing strategy. We argue that consumer income is going to affect responses to pricing strategies such that some consumers are more responsive to a retailer's pricing strategies than others. Previous research indicates that higher income households have higher opportunity costs of time and are less price sensitive (Boatwright, Dhar, and Rossi 2004). As such, consumers with greater buying power, that are less price sensitive and therefore less concerned about where to shop, will be less affected by inconsistent or unclear pricing strategies than people with lower buying power. Furthermore, one of the negative consequences of a hybrid pricing strategy is the inability to offset the costs of price promotions and discounts without charging higher prices. This will be less of a concern in areas of greater buying power because of the lack of price sensitive consumers and therefore lower rates of cherry pickers than in geographic areas with highly price sensitive consumers. As such, we expect that the nonlinear relationship between pricing strategy alignment and retailer sales performance will weaken as the potential customers have increased buying power. More formally, we hypothesize:

> H_{3a}: *With increasing buying power in the region, the U-shaped relationship between a retailer's pricing strategy alignment and the sales dollars per sqm for the retailer weakens.*

> H_{3b}: *With increasing buying power in the region, the U-shaped relationship between a retailer's pricing strategy alignment and the sales volume per sqm for the retailer weakens.*

Population Density. Following the work of Becker (1965) as well as of Gauri, Trivedi, and Grewal (2008), we argue that there is a relationship between disutility for travel and a consumer's choice of retailer. Consumers, on average, have a strong disutility for travel. They will pay more to conserve time and they place a greater value on time-saving options when they perceive their time as especially valuable. In metropolitan areas, i.e. areas of high population density, there is a greater quantity of options in a smaller area, and therefore there is a lower cost of visiting different retail stores. We argue that this will moderate the negative consequences of a hybrid pricing strategy. As previously indicated, a hybrid pricing strategy suffers in situations where consumer uncertainty deters patronage. This consequence is likely to be more severe in rural areas, relative to metropolitan areas, because the cost of traveling to multiple stores in a rural area is much greater. In rural areas consumers will be less willing to visit multiple stores, and therefore will have a desire to patron stores with which they have *confidence* and are *certain* about the pricing and value the store offers. As such, we argue that the negative impact of hybrid strategies will be less apparent in metropolitan areas, i.e., areas with higher population density. More formally, we argue:

> H_{4a}: *With increasing population density, the U-shaped relationship between a retailer's pricing strategy alignment and the sales dollars per sqm for the retailer weakens.*

> H_{4b}: *With increasing population density, the U-shaped relationship between a retailer's pricing strategy alignment and the sales volume per sqm for the retailer weakens.*

3.2.4.2 Store factors

"Store format" is recognized as a key part of a retail strategy (Gauri, Trivedi, and Grewal 2008). However it is noted that, despite the integral role that store format plays, there is limited research that investigates "the strategic selection of price and format policies" (p. 256, Gauri, Trivedi, and Grewal 2008). In this research we offer some initial insight into the role of store format by investigating a key store format variable: discounter versus non-discounter.

Store format: Discounter vs. Non-Discounter. Consumers form expectations about a store's pricing based on whether the store is a discounter or non-discounter. However, the *actual pricing strategy* of the store does not always match these expectations. More specifically, in the German retail market discounters are expected to follow an EDLP strategy whereas supermarkets and non-discounters are expected to follow a Hi-Lo strategy and offer several price promotions. However, there are instances in which a supermarket follows a strategy more closely related to an EDLP pricing strategy and does not offer many price promotions. For example, a well-known German grocery retailer mostly follows pricing strategies closely aligned with Hybrid and EDLP even though its classification as a non-discounter would suggest otherwise.

Despite the fact that the retailer may or may not be using a pricing strategy that is associated with its store format, these images are prevalent and therefore consumers have expectations about pricing. These images impact the performance of the strategy that the retailer is *actually pursuing*. Discounters maintain a low-price image in the mind of the consumer (Van Heerde, Gijsbrechts, and Pauwels 2008). On the other hand, non-discounters are expected to focus on a Hi-Lo pricing strategy where they offer frequent price promotions. We argue that a departure from the "expected" pricing strategy is likely to be more easily tracked and therefore receive a more negative response from consumers in the case of non-discounters versus discounters. In other words, if consumers expect promotional activities on a regular basis (which is what they expect from non-discounters), then they are likely to notice when a retailer deviates by offering fewer price discounts and less promotional activities. The salience and ease of observation of promotional activities makes a hybrid pricing strategy more harmful for a non-discounter versus a discounter. As such, non-discounters, relative to discounters, are likely to be more heavily penalized for moving toward a hybrid strategy. More formally, we hypothesize:

H_{5a}: *Compared to non-discounters, the U-shaped relationship between a retailer's pricing strategy alignment and the sales dollars per sqm for the retailer weakens for discounters.*

H_{5b}: *Compared to non-discounters, the U-shaped relationship between a retailer's pricing strategy alignment and the sales volume per sqm for the retailer weakens for discounters.*

3.2.4.3   Competitive factors

Prior research suggests that retail competition is an important determinant of retail pricing (Chintagunta 2002; Ellickson and Misra 2008; Lal and Villas-Boas 1998). In addition, research indicates that retailers are very sensitive to the activities of their competitors in the same market (Hanssens 1980; Lambin, Naert and Bultez 1975). In fact, Shankar and Bolton (2004) show that competitor factors are the most dominant factor influencing retailer pricing strategy among several other factors. Furthermore, we know from our expert interviews that competitors have a big influence on the retailer's pricing strategy. As such, it is likely that the competitive environment impacts the effectiveness of a retailer's pricing strategy.

Competitive Intensity. Competition provides consumers with options and opportunities to take their dollars elsewhere. As such, in conditions of increased competitive intensity – in terms of number of competitors in the same zip-code area – it is even more important to provide consumers with a clear image of the retailer's pricing strategy and have an effective pricing strategy. Hybrid strategies are vulnerable to attacks from competitors that follow pure strategies (Thornhill and White 2007). Moreover, hybrid strategies are "common and occupy a heavily contested or crowded region of strategic space – a situation unlikely to result in high performance" (Thornhill and White 2007). In other words, when consumers have more options then weaker retail pricing strategies, such as the hybrid pricing strategy, will become even more vulnerable and the poor performance will be even more pronounced. More formally, we hypothesize:

H_{6a}: *As competitive intensity in the region increases, the U-shaped relationship between a retailer's pricing strategy alignment and the sales dollars per sqm for the retailer strengthens.*

H_{6b}: *As competitive intensity in the region increases, the U-shaped relationship between a retailer's pricing strategy alignment and the sales volume per sqm for the retailer strengthens.*

3.3 Method

3.3.1 Empirical context and data

The data we use for our study is objective weekly scanner data collected at the store-level and obtained from SymphonyIRI Group in Germany. The data covers a two-year period (2009-2010) and contains in total over thirteen million data points. It includes 931 retail stores, which is an extensive representation of the German grocery retailing market. The sample includes both grocery retailers and drug stores. To measure our moderating and control variables, we obtained additional data from the GfK Germany, the German Federal Statistical Office and www.supermarktcheck.de.

The data include a product basket with the following 34 categories: deodorant, shampoo, chocolate bars, shower gel, coffee, margarine, cream cheese, general purpose cleaner, yogurt, pralines, liqueur, sparkling wine/champagne, salty snacks, rice, cereal, soups/stew, sausage and cold meat, auto dish, total hand & body care, heavy duty detergent, sweet spread, ketchup, chocolate/cereal bars, alcoholic beverages, fruit gums, pizza, air freshener, brandy cognac, tooth paste, dog food, bathroom tissue, juice, soft drinks and instant soups/ready to eat meals. For each category the four to seven major brands/products (in terms of revenue) were included in the database. To ensure the product basket was representative, we compared it to the shopping basket of the German Federal Statistical Office. Furthermore, when choosing the categories we collaborated closely with the category experts at the

SymphonyIRI office in Düsseldorf, Germany. To ensure that we had variation in pricing strategy alignment that represented a realistic retail store, we included both products with deep and frequent price reductions as well as products that are not often or not as deeply reduced in price.

3.3.2 Measures

3.3.2.1 Focal construct: pricing strategy alignment

To measure the focal construct *Pricing Strategy Alignment*, wherever possible we used existing measures and adapted them to our context (cf. Bolton and Shankar 2003; Hoch, Dreze, and Purk 1994; Voss and Seiders 2003). We conceptualize pricing strategy alignment in terms of three dimensions: (1) price variation, (2) deal intensity and (3) deal support. Based on previous research we identify one item for price variation and three items for both deal intensity and deal support. As such, there are seven items, which represent three dimensions, included in our measurement of pricing strategy alignment.

The first dimension, *price variation*, is reflected by one item. This item is calculated using the ratio of the standard deviation of the price and the mean of the price (Bolton and Shankar 2003). This item is calculated first for all products over the two years 2009 and 2010 in each of the 34 categories, resulting in around 187 measures (assumption: in average 5,5 products per category; 5,5 products x 34 categories). Then, the 5,5 product measures in each of the 34 category are aggregated up to the category level using mean values, resulting in 34 measures for the first dimension—price variation.

The second dimension, *deal intensity*, is reflected by three items: (a) the average deal depth across all weeks, (b) the average deal depth across only deal weeks and (c) the percentage of weeks with deals (Bolton and Shankar 2003). These three items are each calculated first for all products over two years for each of the 34 categories, resulting in 3 x 187 = 561 measures. Then, the 5,5 product measures in each of the 34 category are aggregated up to the category level using mean values, resulting in 34 measures for (a) the average deal depth across all weeks, 34 measures for (b) the average deal depth across only deal weeks and 34 measures for (c) the percentage of weeks with deals. In total, we got 3 x 34 = 102 measures for the second dimension—deal intensity.

The final dimension, *deal support*, is reflected by three items: (a) percentage of weeks with feature and deal, (b) percentage of weeks with display and deal and (c) percentage of weeks with feature, display and deal (Bolton and Shankar 2003). These three items are each calculated first for all products over two years for each of the 34 categories, resulting in 3 x 187 = 561 measures. Then also here, the 5,5 product measures in each of the 34 category Then, the values at the product level are aggregated up to the category level using mean values, resulting in 34 measures for (a) percentage of weeks with feature and deal, 34 measures for (b) percentage of weeks with display and deal and 34 measures for (c) percentage of weeks with feature, display and deal. In total, there are also 3 x 34 = 102 measures for the third dimension—deal support.

In total, we had over 1.300 measures at the product level, which were aggregated in 238 measures at the category level:

- 34 measures for the first dimension "price variation"
- 102 measures for the second dimension "deal intensity"
- 102 measures for the third dimension "deal support".

Then the dimension "price variation" was built by aggregating the 34 measures through principal component analysis. As it consists of only one item, no further aggregation is necessary to achieve the final dimension value. The dimension "deal intensity" was built by first aggregating the 34 measures for each of its three items through principal component analysis and finally aggregating the remaining three measures to the dimension "deal intensity". The dimension "deal support" was built by first aggregating the 34 measures for each of its three items through principal component analysis and finally aggregating the remaining three measures to the dimension "deal support".

The aggregation process from the very detailed EAN-level or product level up to the category level and finally to the store level is very complex. Therefore the steps of the aggregation process are summarized in the following:

1. **EAN/product level measures:** Each single measure is first calculated for an individual EAN/product for one week within a single product category.
2. **Category level measures:** Then, these product measures are aggregated over the whole time period of the years 2009 and 2010. We calculate every measure consistently over the 2-year period from 2009 to 2010. After that, the product measures are aggregated up to the category-level by building mean scores.
3. **Store level measures:** To achieve store-level measures, the category measures for all 34 categories are aggregated using principal component analysis.
4. **Store level dimensions:** The dimension "price variation" consists of only one measure. Therefore no further aggregation is necessary to achieve the dimension level. The dimension "deal intensity" consists of three measures. We therefore aggregate these three measures to achieve the dimension "deal intensity" by using principal component analysis. The dimension "deal support" also consists of three measures. Therefore, we also aggregate the

three measures by using principal component analysis to get the dimension "deal support".

5. **Store level construct:** Finally, we aggregate the three dimensions "price variation", "deal intensity" and "deal support" using principal component analysis to create our focal construct pricing strategy alignment.

In summary, we calculated the measures from the product level up to the category level and finally to the product basket level, which is essential in order to represent the store-level. Furthermore, through this aggregation process, we follow the suggestion of prior research to build a more comprehensive measure of pricing strategy (Voss and Seiders 2003). Figure 4 shows the aggregation process.

The histogram depicting pricing strategy alignment is shown in Figure 5. The histogram shows, that most of the retailers in our sample have a moderate level of pricing strategy alignment whereby they use a hybrid pricing strategy and are not clearly aligned with either EDLP or Hi-Lo. The minority of the retailers in the sample show a clear focus on either EDLP or Hi-Lo.

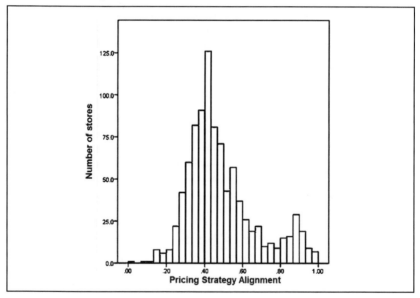

Figure 5:   Histogram of pricing strategy alignment

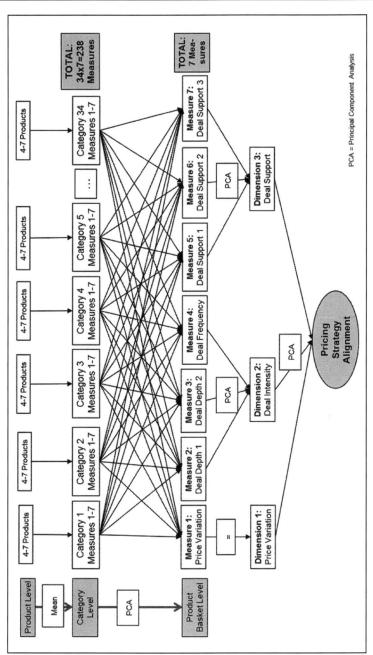

Figure 4: Measurement model of pricing strategy alignment

In figure 5, we plotted the final focal construct pricing strategy alignment on a scale between 0 and 1 in order to show how the construct is distributed. The original values of pricing strategy alignment resulting from the principal component analysis range between 0 and 7.93 and the final measure has a mean of zero.

3.3.2.2 Performance variables

We include both sales dollars (Mulhern and Leone 1990) and sales volume (Hoch, Dreze, and Purk 1994) as performance outcomes of pricing strategy in retailing. In order to make our dependent variable comparable across different types of stores, we scale it relative to the size of the store. We calculate sales dollars per sqm [€] and sales volume per sqm [Unit] by dividing the sum of sales dollars/sales volume over products, category and product baskets by the amount of squaremeters of the store. We have intervals of the store sizes given in the data and use the means to have an exact amount of squaremeters by store. The data used to create these measures were obtained from the SymphonyIRI data.

3.3.2.3 Moderating variables

Buying Power. Buying Power was obtained from GfK Germany and was measured as per capita index per zip code. The measure was matched to the original data set of SymphonyIRI. The GfK buying power is the acknowledged benchmark for assessing consumption potential. It shows where the regions with the highest buying power are found. Buying power is determined directly at the place where the consumer lives and therefore is an important indicator of the consumption potential of the local population. The bases for the GfK buying power are official wage and income tax statistics, economic information from financial institutions and economic forecasts for the current year. In general, a buying power of <90 means that the consumption potential in the region or zip code area is rather low, whereas a buying power of >110 means that the consumption potential in the region or zip code area is rather high.

Population Density. The population density is the average number of inhabitants for a particular area (state, region or the like), usually specified in inhabitants per km². It is calculated by dividing the population of the area by the land mass of the region. This measure was obtained per zip code from the website of the German Federal Statistical Office and was also matched with the original SymphonyIRI data.

Store Format: Discounters vs Non-Discounters. This measure is a dummy variable where discounters are given the score of 1 and non-discounters are given the score of 0. We obtain information on the store format from the SymphonyIRI data. The IRI data contained a classification of the stores into four types: discounter, drug store, traditional supermarket and convenience store. As also agreed with our expert interviewees, we build two groups – discounters and non-discounters – out of the four IRI groups. Thereby we allocated the IRI discounters to the group "discounters" and the IRI drug stores, traditional supermarkets and convenience markets to the group "non-discounters".

Competitive Intensity. Following Shankar and Bolton (2004) we measured competitive intensity using a count of the number of competitors/retailers listed in the same zip code as the focal retailer. We collected this information using the website www.supermarktcheck.de. This website lists all supermarkets and drug stores by zip code. For each zip code (listed in the SymphonyIRI data) we compiled a set of all retailers. This set of retailers was used to identify how many competitors a retailer faced in their particular zip code. We used a filter to exclude non-relevant retailers such as DIY stores, liqueur stores, etc. As such, the set of competitors only included the type of retailers that are in our sample—grocery stores (both discounters and non-discounters) and drug stores.

The descriptive statistics for all of the variables in our model are shown in table 8.

Table 8: Descriptive statistics of variables

	M	SD	(1)	(2)	(3)	(4)	(5)	(6)	(7)
(1) Pricing Strategy Alignment	.00	1.00	1.00						
(2) Sales Dollars/sqm	371.95	216.32	-.16**	1.00					
(3) Sales Volume/sqm	238.22	141.72	-.14**	.99**	1.00				
(4) Buying Power	99.00	15.31	.04	.13**	.14**	1.00			
(5) Population Density	656.88	926.42	-.00	.10**	.07*	.05	1.00		
(6) Discounter	.15	.35	-.35**	.01	.04	-.06	-.07*	1.00	
(7) Number of Competitors	88.17	62.29	-.05	-.01	-.01	-.05	.14**	.05	1.00

* p < .05; ** p < .01; Score of pricing strategy alignment based on the principal component analysis; measure of sales dollars (actual values are in Euro) and sales volume are per store (for 4-7 products in 34 categories) aggregated over the 2 year period; measures for buying power are at the zip code level (score of 100 is the base score of buying power, scores over 110 are high, scores under 90 are low); measure of population density is inhabitants per square-kilometer at the zip code level; Discounter is a binary variable; measure of number of competitors is at the zip code level.

3.4 Results

3.4.1 Analysis approach

To test our theoretical framework we use a random-effects estimation. This estimation technique is appropriate because it accounts for the multiple stores that may represent one given retailer (Greene 2000). In fact, our 931 retailer stores represent 36 different retail companies and using a random-effects estimation controls for the repeated observations within a given retail chain. We create dummy variables for the 36 retail companies and include it in the random effects model. A Hausman test supports our use of a random-effects model rather than a fixed-effects model (χ^2_{14}=12.77, p=0.55).

The final models that we estimate are the following:

$$SDSQM = \beta_0 + \beta_1 PSA_i + \beta_2 PSA^2_i + \beta_3 PSA_i*BP_i + \beta_4 PSA_i*PD_i + \beta_5 PSA_i*Disc_i + \beta_6 PSA^2_i*Comp_i + \beta_7 PSA^2_i*BP_i + \beta_8 PSA^2_i*PD_i + \beta_9 PSA^2_i*Disc_i + \beta_{10} PSA^2_i*Comp_i + \beta_{11}BP_i + \beta_{12}PD_i + \beta_{13}Disc_i + \beta_{14}Comp_i + \varepsilon_i$$

$$SVSQM = \beta_0 + \beta_1 PSA_i + \beta_2 PSA^2_i + \beta_3 PSA_i*BP_i + \beta_4 PSA_i*PD_i + \beta_5 PSA_i*Disc_i + \beta_6 PSA^2_i*Comp_i + \beta_7 PSA^2_i*BP_i + \beta_8 PSA^2_i*PD_i + \beta_9 PSA^2_i*Disc_i + \beta_{10} PSA^2_i*Comp_i + \beta_{11}BP_i + \beta_{12}PD_i + \beta_{13}Disc_i + \beta_{14}Comp_i + \varepsilon_i$$

Where: i is the individual retailer, $SDSQM$ is the sales dollars per squaremeter, $SVSQM$ is the sales volume per squaremeter, PSA is the focal construct "Pricing Strategy Alignment", BP is Buying Power, PD is Population Density, $Disc$ is Discounter dummy, and $Comp$ is competitive intensity.

We report the estimation results of the models with the two dependent variables (sales dollars per squaremeter and sales volume per squaremeter) in columns 1 and 2 of table 9 respectively.

Table 9:   *Results of model estimation*

	Sales Dollars/sqm		Sales Volume/sqm	
	Estimate	(Standard Error)	Estimate	(Standard Error)
Focal Construct				
Pricing Strategy Alignment	-86.12***	(14.13)	-48.80***	(9.24)
Pricing Strategy Alignment^2	19.28**	(8.32)	12.56**	(5.43)
Interaction Terms				
Pricing Strategy Alignment^2*Buying Power	26.50***	(8.69)	16.97***	(5.65)
Pricing Strategy Alignment^2*Population Density	6.50	(8.77)	3.83	(5.70)
Pricing Strategy Alignment^2* Discounter	-134.33**	(67.79)	-91.00**	(44.02)
Pricing Strategy Alignment^2*Competitive Intensity	-6.13	(8.37)	-3.89	(5.44)
Control Variables				
Pricing Strategy Alignment*Buying Power	-39.90***	(8.49)	-26.25***	(5.51)
Pricing Strategy Alignment*Population Density	-7.11	(7.96)	-4.39	(5.17)
Pricing Strategy Alignment*Discounter	-274.70***	(84.91)	-187.61***	(55.13)
Pricing Strategy Alignment*Competitive Intensity	4.90	(7.75)	3.56	(5.04)
Buying Power	24.20***	(6.28)	17.94***	(4.08)
Population Density	14.50**	(6.44)	7.53**	(4.18)
Discounter	-278.30***	(98.70)	-173.58***	(64.96)
Competitive Intensity	-5.92	(6.31)	-3.85	(4.10)
Intercept (β_0)	348.89***	(24.72)	217.93***	(16.64)
N	931		931	
R^2	0.095		0.084	

* p < .10; ** p < .05; *** p < .01; unstandardized coefficient estimates and standard errors.

To test the validity of the proposed conceptual framework, we compare the model fit of our model against a baseline model that includes retailer dummies and control variables, but not our focal construct. Using a random-effects model fitted with the maximum likelihood estimator we find improvement in fit using our proposed model compared to the baseline model ($AIC_{proposed}$=12383 compared to $AIC_{baseline}$=12451; $BIC_{proposed}$=12465 compared to $BIC_{baseline}$=12485). The fit statistics for our estimated models also indicate that they fit the data well (χ^2_{14}=113.57, p <0.01 for sales dollars per sqm; χ^2_{14}=107.65, p< 0.01 for sales volume per sqm) with an R^2 of 0.095 for sales dollars per sqm, and an R^2 of 0.084 for sales volume per sqm.

We find support for H_1, indicating a nonlinear, U-shaped relationship between pricing strategy alignment and sales dollars per sqm (β_1 = -86.12, p < 0.01; β_2 = 19.28, p < 0.05). This suggests that to be more effective, i.e., to have greater sales dollars per sqm, a retailer should use one of the generic pricing strategies rather than a hybrid pricing strategy. In addition, we found support for H_2, indicating a nonlinear U-shaped relationship between pricing strategy alignment and sales volume per sqm (β_1 = -48.80, p < 0.01; β_2 = 12.56, p < 0.05). This suggests that to be more effective, i.e., to have greater sales volume per sqm, a retailer should use one of the generic pricing strategies rather than a hybrid pricing strategy. Our support of both hypotheses H_1 and H_2 give overall support to the idea that getting "stuck in the middle" when it comes to pricing strategies can have poor sales performance implications for retailers.

We also find evidence that this relationship is contingent on other factors. We find evidence that buying power moderates the relationship between pricing strategy alignment and firm performance. Interestingly it is in the opposite direction than hypothesized in H_{3a-b} (β_1 = -39.90, p < 0.01 ; β_2 = 26.50, p < 0.01; for sales dollars per sqm; and β_1 = -26.25, p < 0.01 ; β_2 = 16.97, p < 0.01 for sales volume per sqm). This suggests that as buying power in the region increases, the non-linear relationship between pricing strategy alignment and sales performance strengthens. In other words, the difference between focusing on one or the other pricing strategy, as opposed to using a hybrid, becomes greater such that the negative impact of using a hybrid strategy becomes even more pronounced. Figure 6 shows the significant marginal effect of the buying power on the relationship between pricing strategy alignment and both sales performance variables.

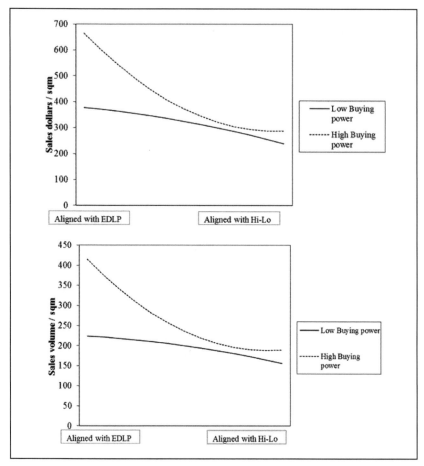

*Figure 6:   Marginal effect of buying power on the relationship between pricing strategy
              alignment and sales performance*

We do not find support for H_{4a-b}. Based on the insignificant estimates of the interaction terms we conclude that population density does not have a moderating effect on the relationship between retail pricing strategy and sales performance. This suggests that in both metropolitan and rural areas there are negative implications for following a hybrid pricing strategy, however this effect does not differ across the two levels of population density.

We find support for our hypotheses H_{5a-b}. This suggests that compared to non-discounters, the non-linear relationship between pricing strategy alignment and sales dollars per sqm (as well as sales volume per sqm) weakens for discounters (β_1 = -274.70, p < 0.01; β_2 =-134.33, p < 0.05 ; (β_1 = -187.61, p < 0.01 ; β_2 = -91.00, p < 0.05). Figure 7 shows the significant marginal effect of the store format on the relation between pricing strategy alignment and both sales performance variables.

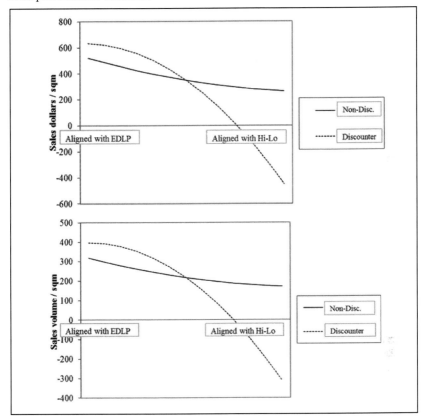

*Figure 7:   Marginal effect of store format on the relationship between pricing strategy
            alignment and sales performance*

Finally, we do not find support for H_{6a-b}. Based on the insignificant estimates of the interaction terms we conclude that competitive intensity does not have a moderating effect on the relationship between retail pricing strategy and sales performance. This suggests that the negative effects of a hybrid pricings strategy do not get worse with more intense competition.

3.4.2 Additional analysis

In order to test the robustness checks of our presented results we conducted additional analyses whereby we used cluster analysis to show the underlying pricing strategies.

Cluster Analysis to Validate Aggregation. The decision to aggregate the three dimensions and create one variable – pricing strategy alignment – was based on the fundamental goal of understanding an overall pricing strategy, versus pricing decisions. While understanding how each of those dimensions impacts store performance is very important, it is also important to understand how those dimensions *work together* to impact store performance. The need to understand this holistic view was echoed by the managers we interviewed who wanted to understand "the big picture comparison of Hi-Lo versus EDLP pricing strategies" as well as the desire to understand "the effectiveness of an overall pricing strategy". Despite the deductive and inductive reasoning that led us to measure our focal construct as one measure on a continuum, we wanted to test the robustness of this aggregated measure. To do so, we tested for clusters using the decomposed dimensions – price variation, deal intensity and deal support. Table 10 shows the results of the cluster analysis, including descriptive statistics – mean values of sales dollars per sqm, sales volume per sqm, store size, number of competitors, buying power in the region and population density – for each cluster.

Table 10: Results from the cluster analysis with the dimensions of pricing strategy alignment

Cluster Number (size)	Dimensions				Descriptive Statistics					
	Pricing Strategy	Price Variation	Deal Intensity	Deal Support	Sales dollars [€/sqm]	Sales volume [unit/sqm]	Store size [sqm]	No. of competitors	Buying Power	Population Density
1 (140)	Strong Hi-Lo (15%)	0.93 (high)	0.83 (high)	0.65 (high)	373.1	248.7	6996.7	80.3	100.8	620.4
2 (513)	High Hybrid (55%)	0.80 (high)	0.42 (low)	0.22 (low)	412.9	260.7	1845.0	87.7	99.7	668.2
3 (132)	Low Hybrid (14%)	0.49 (moderate)	0.60 (moderate)	0.52 (moderate)	214.2	130.1	363.5	91.9	97.3	794.9
4 (146)	Strong EDLP (16%)	0.30 (low)	0.41 (low)	0.25 (low)	369.7	246.9	687.5	94.1	96.5	526.9

* Based on the total sample of 931 stores. Low, moderate and high labels are based on mean scores for each dimension. measure of sales dollars (actual values are in Euro) and sales volume are per store (for 4-7 products in 34 categories) aggregated over the 2 year period; measures for buying power are at the zip code level (score of 100 is the base score of buying power, scores over 110 are high, scores under 90 are low); measure of population density is inhabitants per square-kilometer at the zip code level; Discounter is a binary variable; measure of number of competitors is at the zip code level.

The results show that the data can be best represented by four clusters: One cluster can be interpreted to represent "strong Hi-Lo", the second as "high hybrid", and the third cluster represents "low hybrid" and the fourth cluster reflects "strong EDLP". As such, it suggests that indeed the pricing strategy in retailing is well represented using a continuum where "strong EDLP" and "strong HiLo" are the ends of the continuum and hybrid pricing strategies in between.

3.5 Discussion of results

To our knowledge, this is the first study that measures and compares retail pricing strategies at the store-level using objective scanner data. It is very important to note that despite the fact that most retailers are pursuing hybrid pricing strategies, there has not been an empirical or theoretical test to answer how a hybrid pricing strategy impacts store sales performance. We find that there is a nonlinear relationship between pricing strategy alignment and retailers' sales dollars and sales volume per sqm. Quite simply, we show for the first time that grocery retailers should avoid getting stuck in the middle when it comes to pricing strategies; retailers are better off pursuing either a Hi-Lo or an EDLP pricing strategy. Our study contributes to the understanding of retail pricing for both researchers and managers in marketing.

3.5.1 Theoretical implications

This research is the first to (i) conduct a comprehensive examination of pricing *strategies* (as opposed to pricing tactics); (ii) investigate the outcomes of pricing strategies from a *retailer's perspective*, i.e., examining retailer performance outcomes; and (iii) offer insight at the *store-level*. In doing so, this research makes two distinct distinct contributions to the literature in marketing. First, our research provides a comprehensive measurement of the extent to which a store aligns with one of the generic pricing strategies, versus following a hybrid pricing strategy. While prior research has examined the effects of individual dimensions of a pricing strategy (e.g., price variation) (Bolton and Shankar 2003), this is the first to aggregate the dimensions into one construct. This aggregated, or holistic, construct is important. As noted by the experts we interviewed, a long-term strategy needs to be set for an entire store. More specifically, if a retailer wants to optimize their store's performance, it is important to understand how all of the pricing dimensions work together to impact store performance. For example, consider a store where there are two category managers each using a different pricing strategy. Empirical analyses at the category level could provide results that indicate that this is an optimal pricing strategy. However, our findings show that when you analyze this at the store level, as suggested be done by the managers we interviewed, it is likely to be suboptimal. Using our store-level measure we find that using two different pricing strategies within one store can have detrimental effects on the store's overall sales performance.

Second, our research adds to the ongoing investigation as to how hybrid, versus aligned, strategies affect important performance outcomes. Following Porter (1980), we postulate a U-shaped relationship between pricing strategy alignment and the performance outcomes. Our results show that when the dimensions of pricing strategy alignment are consistent, i.e., are all together either have a relatively high score or a relatively low score and therefore result in one strong pricing strategy, a retailer has much greater firm performance than when the individual dimensions are inconsistent and a retailer follows a hybrid strategy. Our results are in line with the theory of Porter in his generic competitive strategies: a firm that is not able to develop its strategy in one clear direction is "stuck in the middle".

While our findings have specific implications for retailer pricing strategy, there are also broader implications for the effects of hybrid strategies in general. Our research highlights the importance of strategic synergies and consistent messaging that result from pursuing an aligned strategy, as opposed to the benefits that might come from diversifying or using multiple tactics that result from pursuing a hybrid strategy. These findings can also have implications for other types of firms and other strategic decisions. For example, it would be worthy of investigating how our arguments pertain to a firm facing the trade-offs of focusing on an exploration versus exploitation market development strategy. Would being completely aligned with one of these strategies be better because it creates synergies or would a hybrid strategy be more optimal?

3.5.2 Managerial implications

We examine the effect of pricing strategy alignment on retailer sales performance, as well as test the moderating effects between pricing strategy alignment and performance. Several characteristics of our study make it insightful for managers. First, our empirical analysis was conducted in the retailing industry, which is an under-examined industry with regard to pricing strategies. Pricing strategies have been examined in the online environment, in the university setting, as well as from the manufacturer's perspective (Ho and

Wang 2011; Kocas and Bohlmann 2008; Routroy and Singh 2011). However, this study provides insight for managers in the retailing industry, a relatively less investigated context for understanding overall pricing strategies.

Second, our investigation is at the store-level which provides helpful and unique insights for managers. As one of the experts in our qualitative study noted, "The basic decision about a pricing strategy – Hi-Lo or EDLP – has to be done at the store level. A pricing strategy cannot easily be done product by product". Through this research we discovered that managers want to understand consequences at the store level, because they have the important task of setting the strategic direction for their retail stores, including training employees, determining incentive structures, and allocating pivotal resources. Our research provides insight to managers trying to make these decisions for their firms because it suggests that setting incentives to optimize category-level performance may reduce the benefits of marketing synergies in the store and may result in inconsistent messaging, both of which negatively affect the overall store performance.

Third, our findings have actionable implications for managers. Our qualitative research made it clear that managers, even those in the C-suite, are interested in knowing the answer to whether or not they should focus on a specific retail pricing strategy. Our findings have clear implications for these managers: our descriptive results show, that around 75% of the German retailers are pursuing a hybrid pricing strategy in between EDLP and Hi-Lo. Our empirical results show that this is not the best solution: retailers should focus on either a strong EDLP or a strong High-Low pricing strategy in order to be more successful in terms of sales dollars per sqm and sales volume per sqm – we show that retailers that get "stuck in the middle" diminish their sales dollars per sqm [€] and sales volume per sqm [Unit] compared to retailers with a clear focus pricing strategy. This means that retail managers should make a clear decision which pricing strategy to follow in order to convey a clear image to the consumer.

The findings from our moderating effects also have several interesting implications. First, the buying power in the region has a significant positive impact on this U-shaped relationship between pricing strategy alignment and performance outcomes. This suggests that for retailers operating in areas where the potential consumers have high incomes they should be even more motivated not to pursue a hybrid pricing strategy. As such, retailers should consider the location of their store in combination with other factors when determining their pricing strategy. Second, the population density in the region has no significant impact on the main effect in our model. Therefore, we suggest that a retailer should focus less on the concentration or density of people living in the neighborhood of the store, and instead should focus on the buying power of those people. Third, our results suggest that for non-discounters, relative to discounters, it is even more important to take a clear price position as either aligned with an EDLP or Hi-Lo pricing strategy. We speculate that discounters – in contrast to non-discounters – already have a certain low price image in the mind of the consumer.

3.5.3 Limitations and need for further research

Many of the contributions of this research come from the rich and objective data. However, future research could benefit by testing these research questions with more data. Specifically, profitability measures that include costs in the analysis would provide greater insight into the optimal pricing strategy for retailers. It would be interesting to see if the nonlinear, convex-shaped relationship holds up when the firm performance measure controls for the costs of executing particular pricing strategies.

Another opportunity for future research would be to look at two different scenarios regarding the moderate score of the price promotion activity: (1) inconsistent strategies (EDLP and Hi-Lo) for different categories, or (ii) an inconsistent hybrid pricing strategy for all categories. It could be interesting to study the performance implications for both scenarios, where a hypothesis could be that the consistent hybrid strategy (ii) is less confusing and therefore better than the inconsistent strategy (i).

Future research may additionally benefit from testing more contingency factors. Based on prior research we examined the moderating effects of store, market, and competitive characteristics. However, there are other factors that could also influence the relationship between retailer pricing strategies and firm performance. For example, chain, manufacturer factors, pricing history and costs have been identified as possible factors that could influence the pricing strategy in retailing (Nijs, Srinivasan, and Pauwels 2007; Shankar and Bolton 2004; Tellis 1986). Future research that has access to data to measure these variables would provide additional insight into understanding the relationship between pricing strategy alignment and firm performance.

Furthermore, the impact of consumers' reference price on the profitability of these strategies, considering the paper of Kopalle et al. (2012), where the authors argue that reference prices have an impact on whether a retailer should use rather an EDLP or a Hi-Lo pricing strategy.

Another fruitful avenue for future research would be to examine the topic of pricing strategies in retailing at the category level. As also stated by some of our interviewees in our qualitative pre-study, this would be certainly an interesting research field with concrete implications for retail managers with what to do with their categories in terms of pricing and to find out which categories are more appropriate for EDLP, which for Hi-Lo, etc.

The empirical setting of our study provided certain strengths for this study. For example, using the German retailing market was beneficial because it allowed us to have data on the majority of the retailers, making the sample very representative of the market. Furthermore, using the grocery sector of the retail market was beneficial because it is a very lucrative market sector and it provides interesting, yet generalizable findings. However, it may be useful for future research to replicate the study in a different context to see if the findings hold. For example, testing the theoretical framework in different countries might reveal differences or testing the theoretical framework in different retail sectors such as fashion, DIY stores or consumer electronics, may reveal differences. It would be interesting to see if hybrid pricing strategies are more or less effective in different retail sectors.

Furthermore one could probably address an endogeneity discussion, as market conditions certainly play a role in the choice of a pricing strategy of a retailer. While the chains with strong market power are able to choose clear positioning strategies, struggling and smaller firms may try to be both because they are not able to compete with the leading retailers in the market. They may try to be differentiating from the pure strategy firms. In our study we included the competitor situation, but still the influence of further market conditions could be worthwhile to include in future studies about this topic.

For future research it may also be interesting to have a closer look at the three underlying dimensions "price variation", "deal intensity" and "deal support" of our focal construct. The correlation matrix of these three dimensions reveals that there is a weak linear relation between "price variation" and "deal intensity" and between "price variation" and "deal support", but a medium linear relation between "deal intensity" and "deal support". Therefore, maybe future research could exchange either deal intensity or deal support by another reasonable dimension such as "price level" for example.

4 Price Promotion Activity at the Category Level: Less is More?[4]

4.1 Introduction

We base this study on the theoretical foundations from chapter 2 and the methodological foundations from chapter 3. Both chapters 2 and 3 mentioned the limitation that the topic of pricing strategy in retailing should be also examined at the category level. We address this fruitful avenue for future research in the following study.

According to a study of the German "Gesellschaft für Konsumforschung" (GFK) and SAP, the share of price promotions on total sales increased constantly during the last years – independently of economic boom or recession. In German grocery retailing the number of price promotions is currently on a new record-high. Almost every fifth Euro in grocery retailing is now achieved with products that are particularly advertised or offered at reduced price. For example "Milka"-chocolate is offered at discounted prices up to 39 cents for the 100-g bar, Lidl advertises its "Super Saturday" with many price promotions and also Netto and Norma change prices on individual promotion-days. Thereby there is a hazard that through this wide variety of price promotions, even less price-sensitive customers gets used to discounted goods. Customers are educated to pure "price promotion"-buyers, including those that are in principle willing to pay higher prices. Therefore, retailers have to assess the economic viability of their price promotions.

In our qualitative interviews that we conducted also for our study in chapter 3, many interviewees stressed the importance of knowing more about the effect of price promotions on the sales dollars of a retailer at the category level. For example, one manager of a large retailer in Germany stated that although the overall pricing strategy for their retailers is centralized, the single retailers have an influence on the pricing strategy of single categories. Therefore, "it would be interesting to examine the category level with regard to pricing strategies". A CEO of a consulting company said that it would be interesting to see if the retailer says for certain categories: "do I go Hi-Lo or EDLP?". In our following study, we therefore address this important topic and examine the price promotion activity at the category level and its impact on the productivity of the sales area of the retailer.

---

4   Based on an unpublished manuscript of El Husseini/Fassnacht (2012)

4.2 Method

4.2.1 Data

For this study, we use the same data as in our study in chapter 3, containing objective weekly scanner data collected at the store-level and obtained from SymphonyIRI Group in Germany. The data covers a two-year period (2009-2010) and includes 931 retail stores.

The data include the following 34 categories: deodorant, shampoo, chocolate bars, shower gel, coffee, margarine, cream cheese, general purpose cleaner, yogurt, pralines, liqueur, sparkling wine/champagne, salty snacks, rice, cereal, soups/stew, sausage and cold meat, auto dish, total hand & body care, heavy duty detergent, sweet spread, ketchup, chocolate/cereal bars, alcoholic beverages, fruit gums, pizza, air freshener, brandy cognac, tooth paste, dog food, bathroom tissue, juice, soft drinks and instant soups/ready to eat meals. For each category the four to seven major brands/products (in terms of revenue) were included in the database.

4.2.2 Measures

4.2.2.1   Price promotion activity

In chapter 3, we measured the *pricing strategy alignment* at the store level as focal construct. The aggregation process of this construct was described in detail in chapter 3.3.2.1: we aggregated the values of the items from the EAN/product-level up to the category-level and finally to the product/category basket level which represented the store level.

As we want to examine the category-level more detailed in this chapter, we base the measurement of the focal construct *price promotion activity* on the measurement process in chapter 3. Therefore we adapted the measures to our category context and aggregated the values of the items from the EAN/product-level up to the category level. Thus, we conceptualize price promotion activity in terms of three dimensions: (1) price variation, (2) intensity of price reduction and (3) support of price reduction. Based on previous research and our previous study, we use one item for price variation and three items for both the intensity of price reduction and the support of price reduction. As such, there are seven items, which represent three dimensions, included in our measurement of price promotion activity.

The first dimension, *price variation*, is reflected by one item. This item is calculated using the ratio of the standard deviation of the price and the mean of the price (Bolton and Shankar 2003). This item is calculated over all products over the two years 2009 and 2010 for each category. The second dimension, *intensity of the price reduction*, is reflected by three items: (a) the average depth of the price reduction across all weeks, (b) the average depth of the price reduction across only deal weeks and (c) the percentage of weeks with price reduction (Bolton and Shankar 2003). These three items are calculated over all products over two years for each category. The final dimension, *support of the price reduction*, is reflected by three items: (a) percentage of weeks with feature and price reduction, (b) percentage of weeks with display and price reduction and (c) percentage of weeks with feature, display and price reduction (Bolton and Shankar 2003). These three items are calculated over all products over two years for each category.

Similar to the aggregation process in chapter 3, each measure was first calculated for an individual product / EAN for one week within a single product category. Then, these product measures were aggregated to the category-level and over the whole time period the years 2009 and 2010 using mean scores. For every category, the three items of the dimensions "intensity of price reduction" and "support of price reduction" were aggregated through principal component analysis. The dimension "price variation" consists just of one single item so there was no further aggregation necessary. Finally, we aggregated the three dimensions to create "price promotion activity" for each category, also using principal component analysis.

Figure 8 shows the construct price promotion activity as a continuum, resulting in low, middle and high values of price promotion activity.

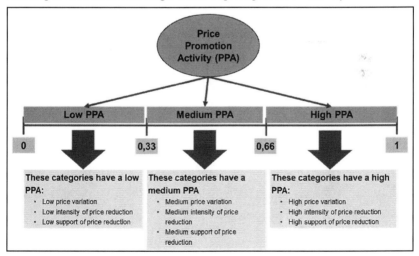

Figure 8:   Price promotion activity as a continuum

4.2.2.2 Productivity of the sales area

To measure our outcome variable – productivity of the sales area – we use the sales dollars per store (Hoch, Dreze, and Purk 1994) and scale it relative to the size of the store, in order to make our dependent variable comparable across different types of stores. We calculate sales dollars per sqm [€] by dividing the sum of sales dollars over products and category by the amount of squaremeters of the store. Thereby, analog to chapter 3, we have intervals of the store sizes given in the data and use the means to have an exact amount of squaremeters by store. The data used to create this measure were also obtained from the SymphonyIRI data.

4.3 Analysis

The final model that we estimate is the following:

$$SDSQM = \beta_0 + \beta_1 PPA_i + \beta_2 PPA^2_i + \varepsilon_i$$

Where: i is the individual retailer, $SDSQM$ is the sales dollars per squaremeter, and PPA is the focal construct "Price Promotion Activity".

To test this model, we use regression analysis, conducted in SPSS. We first examined the quadratic model to test if there is a non-linear relationship between the price promotion activity and the sales dollars per sqm in the store. When the results showed a linear relationship, we used the linear model to test the impact of the construct on the outcome variable.

4.4 Results

We find different relationships between price promotion activity and retailers' sales dollars per sqm:

(1) no relationship,
(2) positive linear relationship,
(3) negative linear relationship,
(4) inverted u-shaped (non-linear) relationship and
(5) u-shaped (non-linear) relationship.

Based on these results, we derive different recommendations for the price promotion activity in each category:

(1) no relationship → recommendation: no PPA
(2) positive linear relationship → recommendation: high PPA
(3) negative linear relationship → recommendation: low PPA

(4) inverted u-shaped (non-linear) relationship → recommendation: medium PPA

(5) u-shaped (non-linear) relationship → recommendation: either high or low PPA

These recommendations are explained in detail in the following chapters 4.4.1 to 4.4.5.

In addition, we evaluate the sales potential per category – dependent on the percentage of the stores, which already follow our PPA-recommendations explained in chapters 4.4.1 to 4.4.5. Thereby, we distinguish four "sales potential"- groups, shown in table 11:

Table 11:   Evaluation of the sales potential per category

Percentage of stores already following our PPA-recommendation	Sales potential (group)
0-25%	Very high (1)
26-50%	High (2)
51-75%	Medium (3)
76-100%	Low (4)

If only 0 – 25% of the stores follow our PPA-recommendation (1) to (5), we see a very high sales potential for this category. If 26 – 50% of the stores follow our PPA-recommendations, we see still a high sales potential for this category. If 51 -75% of the stores follow our PPA-recommendations, we see a medium sales potential and if 76 – 100% follow the PPA-recommendations, there is a low sales potential for the category. If there are several categories within one "sales potential"-group, we conduct an internal group ranking by the respective mean values for the price promotion activity:

(1) Recommendation: no PPA
   • Higher mean values of the price promotion activity indicate a higher sales potential than lower mean values. The higher the mean value, the higher the price promotion activity in this category – and our recommendation is "no PPA". So higher mean values get a higher rank on the "sales potential" scale than lower mean values.

(2) Recommendation: high PPA
   • Lower mean values of the price promotion activity indicate a higher sales potential than higher mean values. The lower the mean value, the lower the price promotion activity in this category – and our

recommendation is "high PPA". So lower mean values get a higher rank on the "sales potential" scale than higher mean values.

(3) Recommendation: low PPA
- Higher mean values of the price promotion activity indicate a higher sales potential than lower mean values. The higher the mean value, the higher the price promotion activity in this category – and our recommendation is "low PPA". So higher mean values get a higher rank on the "sales potential" scale than lower mean values.

(4) Recommendation: medium PPA
- According to figure 8, we define a medium price promotion activity with values between 0.34 and 0.66 on the scale between 0 and 1. Therefore, mean values of the price promotion activity, that are either lower than 0.34 or higher than 0.66, have a higher sales potential than mean values that are closer to or in between this interval.

(5) Recommendation: either high or low PPA
- Medium mean values – interval between 0.34 and 0.66 – of the price promotion activity indicate a higher sales potential than higher or lower mean values. A medium mean value means a medium price promotion activity in this category – and our recommendation is "either high or low PPA". So medium mean values get a higher rank on the "sales potential" scale than higher or lower mean values.

The different recommendations with regard to the price promotion activity and the detailed description of the status quo and sales potential of each category are shown in the following sub-chapters. The categories are named in the order of their classification into to the four "sales potential"-groups. Within the groups, the categories are also named according to their internal group ranking.

4.4.1 Recommendation: No price promotion activity

For the categories in this chapter, the regression analysis showed no significant effect of the price promotion activity on the dollar sales per squaremeter. We therefore recommend generally no price promotion activity for these categories. The detailed results are discussed in the following.

Chocolate/Cereal bars

Our descriptive results show, that 66 % of the stores in our sample follow a low price promotion activity. We therefore classify this category into the "sales potential"- group 3 and derive a medium sales potential for retailers. Retailers should not put any effort in the price promotion activity for this category.

Auto dish

Here we find that already 92.1 % of the stores pursue a low price promotion activity. Therefore, we classify this category into the "sales potential"- group 4 and derive a low sales or cost saving potential in this category. Retailers should stop any remaining price promotion activity for the category auto dish.

4.4.2 Recommendation: High price promotion activity

For the categories in this chapter, the regression analysis showed a significant positive linear effect of the price promotion activity on the dollar sales per squaremeter. We therefore recommend generally a strong price promotion activity for these categories. For every category included in this sub-chapter, we identify a very strong "sales potential". The detailed results are discussed in the following.

Brandy/Cognac

We find that only 0.5 % of the stores in our sample follow a high price promotion activity. We therefore classify this category into the highest "sales potential"- group 1 and derive a very high sales potential for retailers. Retailers should strongly increase the price promotion activity for this category.

Heavy Duty Detergents

Our descriptive results show, that only 9.3 % of the stores in our sample follow a high price promotion activity. We therefore classify this category also into "sales potential"- group 1 and derive a very high sales potential for retailers. Retailers should strongly increase the price promotion activity for this category.

Shower gel

Regarding the category shower gel, 24.3 % of the stores follow a high price promotion activity. Therefore this category is also classified into "sales potential"- group 1 and we derive a very high sales potential for retailers.

Retailers should strongly increase the price promotion activity also for this category.

Shampoo

We find that 24.7 % of the stores follow a high price promotion activity for the category shampoo. We therefore classify this category also into "sales potential"- group 1 and derive a very high sales potential for retailers. Our recommendation is that retailers should strongly increase the price promotion activity for this category.

4.4.3 Recommendation: Low price promotion activity

For the categories in this chapter, the regression analysis showed a significant negative linear effect of the price promotion activity on the dollar sales per squaremeter. We therefore recommend generally a low price promotion activity for these categories. The detailed results are discussed in the following.

Margarine

We find that 22 % of the stores follow a low price promotion activity in this category. We therefore classify this category into "sales potential"- group 1 and derive a very high sales potential for retailers. Retailers should strongly reduce the price promotion activity for the category margarine.

Cream cheese

Our results show that only 12.5 % of the stores pursue a low price promotion activity in this category. We therefore classify this category into "sales potential"- group 1 and derive a very high sales potential for retailers. Retailers should strongly decrease the price promotion activity for the category cream cheese.

Chocolate

36 % of the stores follow a low price promotion activity in this category. We therefore classify this category into "sales potential"- group 2 and derive a high sales potential for retailers. There are still many retailers, pursuing a medium

and high price promotion activity for the category chocolate. Instead, these retailers should strongly diminish the price promotion activity for this category.

Juices

47.5 % of the stores follow a low price promotion activity in this category. We therefore classify this category into "sales potential"- group 2 and derive a high sales potential for retailers. Still more than 50 % of the retailers are pursuing a medium and high price promotion activity for the category juices. Instead, these retailers should strongly diminish the price promotion activity for this category.

Roasted coffee

38.7 % of the stores follow a low price promotion activity in this category. We also classify this category into "sales potential"- group 2 and derive a high sales potential for retailers. Retailers that still pursue a medium or high price promotion activity for the category roasted coffee should instead strongly reduce the price promotion activity for this category.

Yoghurt

62.1 % of the stores follow a low price promotion activity in this category. We therefore classify this category into "sales potential"- group 3 and derive a medium sales potential for retailers in this category. Retailers that still pursue a medium or high level of price promotion activity for the category yoghurt should rather pursue a lower price promotion activity for this category.

Pralines

We find that 65.9 % of the retailers follow a low price promotion activity in this category. Therefore we also classify this category into "sales potential"- group 3 and derive a medium sales potential for retailers in this category. Retailers that still pursue a medium or high level of price promotion activity for the category pralines should rather pursue a lower price promotion activity for this category.

Dog food

We find that 68.8 % of the retailers follow a low price promotion activity in this category. Therefore this category is also classified into "sales potential"- group 3 and we derive a medium sales potential for retailers with regard to category dog food. Stores that still pursue a medium or high level of price promotion activity for the category dog food should follow a lower price promotion activity for this category.

Ham and sausage

We find that already 82.8 % of the stores follow a low price promotion activity in this category. Therefore this category is classified into "sales potential"-group 4 and we derive a low sales potential for retailers with regard to category ham and sausage. The remaining stores that still pursue a medium or high level of price promotion activity should follow a lower price promotion activity for this category.

Soups and stews

We find that already 84.8 % of the stores follow a low price promotion activity in this category. Therefore we classify this category also into "sales potential"-group 4 and we derive a low sales potential for retailers with regard to category soups and stews. The remaining stores that still pursue a medium or high level of price promotion activity should follow a lower price promotion activity for this category.

Salty snacks

We find that already 98.5 % of the stores follow a low price promotion activity in this category. Therefore we classify this category also into "sales potential"-group 4 and we derive a low sales potential for retailers with regard to category salty snacks. There are only 1,5 % of the stores remaining that still pursue a medium or high level of price promotion activity, but the vast majority already follows a low level of price promotion activity.

Air freshener

Already 95.8 % of the stores follow a low price promotion activity in this category. Therefore we classify this category also into "sales potential"- group 4 and we derive a low sales potential for retailers with regard to category air freshener. There are only 4,2 % of the stores remaining that still pursue a medium or high level of price promotion activity, but the vast majority already follows a low level of price promotion activity.

Rice

Already 94 % of the stores follow a low price promotion activity in this category. Therefore this category is also classified into "sales potential"- group 4 and we derive a low sales potential for retailers with regard to category air freshener. There are only 6 % of the stores that still pursue a medium or high level of price promotion activity, but the vast majority already follows a low level of price promotion activity.

4.4.4 Recommendation: Medium price promotion activity

For the categories in this chapter, the regression analysis showed a significant inverted u-shaped (non-linear) relationship between the price promotion activity and the dollar sales per squaremeter. We therefore recommend generally a medium price promotion activity for these categories. The detailed results are discussed in the following.

Bathroom tissue

We find that only 5 % of the stores follow a medium price promotion activity in this category. We classify this category into "sales potential"- group 1 and derive a very high sales potential for retailers. We also find that the majority of 79.6 % of the stores follow a low price promotion activity. These retailers should increase their price promotion activity to a medium level, whereas the remaining retailers that follow a high price promotion activity should rather reduce it.

Soft drinks

We find that 18.7 % of the stores follow a medium price promotion activity in this category. We classify this category also into "sales potential"- group 1 and derive a very high sales potential for retailers. We also find that the majority of 80.2 % of the stores follow a low price promotion activity. These retailers should increase their price promotion activity to a medium level.

Total hand & body care

We find that 11.4 % of the stores follow a medium price promotion activity in this category. We classify this category also into "sales potential"- group 1 and derive a very high sales potential for retailers. Furthermore, we find that the majority of 88.4 % of the stores follow a low price promotion activity. These retailers should increase their price promotion activity to a medium level.

Toothpaste

9.2 % of the stores follow a medium price promotion activity in this category. This category is also classified into "sales potential"- group 1 and we detect a very high sales potential for retailers. We also find that the majority of 88 % of the stores follow a low price promotion activity. We recommend that these retailers should increase their price promotion activity to a medium level, whereas the remaining retailers that follow a high price promotion activity should rather reduce it to achieve an optimal medium level.

Ketchup

We find that 24.1 % of the stores follow a medium price promotion activity in this category. This category is also classified into "sales potential"- group 1 and we derive a very high sales potential for retailers. We also find that 75 % of the stores follow a low price promotion activity. The price promotion activity of these retailers should be increased to a medium level.

Spirituous beverages

20 % of the stores follow a medium price promotion activity in this category. This category is also classified into "sales potential"- group 1 with a very high sales potential for retailers. Besides that, we find that 79.6 % of the stores follow a low price promotion activity. These retailers should raise their price promotion activity to a medium level.

Fruit gums

26.8 % of the stores follow a medium price promotion activity in this category. This category is therefore classified into "sales potential"- group 2 and we derive a high sales potential for retailers. Besides that, 72.2 % of the stores follow a low price promotion activity. These stores should raise their price promotion activity to a medium level.

Cereals

We find that 29.2 % of the stores follow a medium price promotion activity in this category. This category is also classified into "sales potential"- group 2 and we derive a high sales potential for retailers. We also find that 69.9 % of the stores follow a low price promotion activity. The price promotion activity of these stores should be increased to a medium level.

Liquors

Our results show that 27.6 % of the stores follow a medium price promotion activity in this category. This category is also classified into "sales potential"- group 2 and we derive a high sales potential for retailers. We also find that 69.2 % of the stores follow a low price promotion activity. These retailers should increase their price promotion activity to a medium level, whereas the remaining stores that follow a high price promotion activity should reduce it to a medium level.

Instant/convenience food

31.3 % of the stores follow a medium price promotion activity in this category. This category is also classified into "sales potential"- group 2 and we derive a high sales potential for retailers. We also find that 67.7 % of the stores follow a low price promotion activity. These retailers should increase their price promotion activity to a medium level.

Sparkling wine/champaign

47.4 % of the stores follow a medium price promotion activity in this category. This category is also classified into "sales potential"- group 2 and we derive a high sales potential for retailers. We also find that 50.4 % of the stores follow a low price promotion activity. These retailers should increase their price promotion activity to a medium level, whereas the remaining stores that follow a high price promotion activity should reduce it to a medium level.

Sweet spread

We find that 58.5 % of the stores follow a medium price promotion activity in this category. This category is classified into "sales potential"- group 3 and we derive a medium sales potential for retailers. Our results also show that 21 % of the stores follow a low price promotion activity and the remaining 20.5% pursue a high price promotion activity. These retailers should increase, respectively decrease their price promotion activity to a medium level.

Frozen pizza

We find that 74.1 % of the stores follow a medium price promotion activity in this category. We classified this category into "sales potential"- group 3 and derive a medium sales potential for retailers. Furthermore, we detect that 14.4 % of the stores follow a low price promotion activity and the remaining 11.5% pursue a high price promotion activity. These retailers should increase, respectively decrease their price promotion activity to a medium level.

Deodorants

72.4 % of the stores follow a medium price promotion activity in this category. This category is also classified into "sales potential"- group 3 and we derive a medium sales potential for retailers. Furthermore, 20.6 % of the stores follow a low price promotion activity and the remaining 7% pursue a high price promotion activity. These retailers should increase, respectively decrease their price promotion activity to a medium level.

4.4.5 Recommendation: Low *or* high price promotion activity

For the remaining category *general purpose cleaner*, the regression analysis showed a significant u-shaped (non-linear) relationship between the price promotion activity and the dollar sales per squaremeter. We therefore recommend generally rather a low or a high price promotion activity for these categories.

More detailed, 51.9 % of the stores follow a low price promotion activity in this category and 6.6 % follow a high price promotion activity. For the remaining 41.5% of the stores that follow a medium price promotion activity there is a high sales potential. These retailers should decrease, respectively

increase their price promotion activity to an optimal low, respectively high level
of price promotion activity.

4.4.6 Summary of recommendations

The following table 12 gives an overview of the results presented in the previous
chapters 4.4.1 to 4.4.5. It includes the category, status quo of the price
promotion activity and the sales potential.

Table 12:   Overview of the results and recommendations for each category

Recommendation: No price promotion activity		
Category	**Status quo of the price promotion activity of the majority of the stores**	**Sales potential**
Chocolate/ cereal bars SNICKERS	low ⊕⊕ high	• 66% of the stores follow a low price promotion activity • Medium sales potential
Auto Dish Somat	low ⊕ high	• 92.1% of the stores follow a low price promotion activity • Low sales potential
Recommendation: High price promotion activity		
Category	**High price promotion activity already pursued**	**Sales potential**
Brandy/ Cognac		• 0.5% of the stores follow a high price promotion activity • Very high sales potential
Heavy Duty Detergents Persil		• 9.3% of the stores follow a high price promotion activity • Very high sales potential
Shower gels		• 24.3% of the stores follow a high price promotion activity • Very high sales potential
Shampoo		• 23.7% of the stores follow a high price promotion activity • Very high sales potential

Recommendation: Low price promotion activity		
Category	**Low price promotion activity already pursued**	**Sales potential**
Margarine Rama		• 22% of the stores follow a low price promotion activity • Very high sales potential
Cream cheese PHILADELPHIA		• 12.5% of the stores follow a low price promotion activity • Very high sales potential
Chocolate Milka		• 36.3% of the stores follow a low price promotion activity • High sales potential
Juices		• 47.5% of the stores follow a low price promotion activity • High sales potential
Roasted coffee		• 38.7% of the stores follow a low price promotion activity • High sales potential
Yoghurt		• 62.1% of the stores follow a low price promotion activity • Medium sales potential
Pralines		• 65.9% of the stores follow a low price promotion activity • Medium sales potential
Dog Food		• 68.8% of the stores follow a low price promotion activity • Medium sales potential
Ham/ sausage		• 82.8% of the stores follow a low price promotion activity • Low sales potential
Soups/stew		• 84.4% of the stores follow a low price promotion activity • Low sales potential

Category		Sales potential
Salty snacks		• 98.5% of the stores follow a low price promotion activity • Low sales potential
Air freshener		• 95.8% of the stores follow a low price promotion activity • Low sales potential
Rice		• 94% of the stores follow a low price promotion activity • Low sales potential

Recommendation: Medium price promotion activity

Category	Medium price promotion activity already pursued	Sales potential
Bathroom tissue		• 5% of the stores follow a medium price promotion activity • Very high sales potential
Softdrinks		• 18.7% of the stores follow a medium price promotion activity • Very high sales potential
Total Hand& Body Care		• 11.4% of the stores follow a medium price promotion activity • Very high sales potential
Toothpaste		• 9.2% of the stores follow a medium price promotion activity • Very high sales potential
Ketchup		• 24.1% of the stores follow a medium price promotion activity • Very high sales potential
Spirituous beverages		• 20% of the stores follow a medium price promotion activity • Very high sales potential
Fruit gum		• 26.8% of the stores follow a medium price promotion activity • High sales potential

Cereals			• 29.2% of the stores follow a medium price promotion activity • High sales potential
Liquor			• 27.6% of the stores follow a medium price promotion activity • High sales potential
Instant/con-venience food			• 31.3% of the stores follow a medium price promotion activity • High sales potential
Champaign			• 47.4% of the stores follow a medium price promotion activity • High sales potential
Sweet spread			• 58.5% of the stores follow a medium price promotion activity • Medium sales potential
Frozen Pizza			• 74.1% of the stores follow a medium price promotion activity • Medium sales potential
Deodorants			• 72.4% of the stores follow a medium price promotion activity • Medium sales potential

Recommendation: Low _or_ high price promotion activity

Category	Status quo of the price promotion activity of the majority of the stores	Sales potential
General Purpose Cleaner	low ——⊕⊕—— high	• 51.9% of the stores follow a low price promotion activity, 6.6% follow a high price promotion activity • High sales potential for the remaining 41.5% of the stores with a medium price promotion activity

4.5 Discussion

This study analyzes the relationship between the price promotion activity and the sales dollars per squaremeter for 34 categories and 931 German grocery retailers. Our results include several important implications for retail managers. For different categories there are different implications with regard to the price promotion activity. Based on our results, we develop five groups of categories with different managerial implications.

(1) "The golden mean counts"

- Within this group, a medium price promotion activity leads to significantly higher dollar sales per squaremeter. This applies to 41% of the 34 categories in our sample. Among these categories, we have a very high sales potential for bathroom tissues, soft drinks, total hand & body care, tooth paste, ketchup and spirituous beverages. Furthermore, there is a high sales potential for fruit gums, cereals, liquors, instant/convenience food and sparkling wine/champaign. Finally, there is a medium sales potential for sweet spread, frozen pizza and deodorants.

(2) "Less is more"

- Within this group, a lower price promotion activity leads to significantly higher dollar sales per squaremeter. This applies to 38% of the 34 categories in our sample. Among these categories, we have a very high sales potential for margarine and cream cheese. Furthermore, there is a high sales potential for chocolate, juices and roasted coffee. There is a medium sales potential for yoghurt, pralines and dog food. Finally, there is a low sales potential for ham/sausage, soups/stew, salty snacks, air freshener and rice.

(3) "More is more"

- Within this group, a higher price promotion activity leads to significantly higher dollar sales per squaremeter. This applies to 12% of the 34 categories in our sample. Thereby we have a very high sales potential for all of the categories in this group: brandy/cognac, heavy duty detergents, shower gel and shampoo.

(4) "Save your efforts"

- Within this group it does not matter, whether a low, medium or high price promotion activity is followed – it does not have a significant influence on the dollar sales per squaremeter of the store. This applies to two (= 6%) of the 34 categories in our sample. We have a medium sales or cost-saving potential for chocolate/cereal bars and a low sales or cost-saving potential for auto dish.

(5) "Either…or…"

- Within this group of categories there should be a clear focus on either a low or a high price promotion activity. With a medium price promotion activity the store makes the lowest dollar sales per squaremeter. This applies to one (= 3%) of the 34 categories in our sample: general purpose cleaner. Thereby there is a high sales potential for the 41.5% of the stores that pursue a medium price promotion activity for this category.

5 Conclusion

The starting point of this dissertation was the fact that the topic of pricing strategy is one of the top priorities in retail management. Both prior research and the retailing practice gave support for the importance of pricing strategies in retailing: on the one hand, retailing researchers claimed to conduct more research about pricing strategies in retailing – both conceptually and empirically. More concrete, prior research claimed to provide a more detailed understanding of pricing strategy in retailing in terms of definitions, measurement, relevant determinants and retailer specific outcomes. On the other hand, retailing managers that we interviewed in our qualitative pre-study confirmed the importance of this topic in the retailing practice. Despite this importance, until now this topic has been given relatively little attention in the academic research. Therefore, the aim of this work was to provide a better understanding of pricing strategies in retailing both from a theoretical and an empirical perspective. We believe, our work makes three central contributions:

First, it provides a comprehensive examination of the existing literature on pricing strategy in retailing in chapter 2, based on an article of Fassnacht/El Husseini (2012) which has been accepted for publication in the "ZfB – Zeitschrift für Betriebswirtschaft". In this chapter, we examined the existing literature about pricing strategy in retailing with regard to definitions, relevant determinants and outcomes. In total, six conceptual and 21 empirical papers on pricing strategy in retailing were analyzed. Based on the theoretical and conceptual foundations of pricing strategy in retailing, we provided a detailed overview of the different definitions of pricing strategy in retailing and consolidated similarities and differences. Furthermore, we analysed both conceptual and empirical papers about pricing strategy in retailing from all major peer-reviewed journals with regard to determinants and outcomes. Thereby, we detected "market and consumer factors", "retailer factors: assortment, category, store and chain factors", "competitor factors" and "manufacturer and brand factors" as the main groups of determinants of pricing strategy in retailing. Regarding the outcome variables, we found "retailer outcomes" and "customer outcomes" as the two main groups that were covered in prior research. The paper concludes with a comprehensive future research agenda. Thereby, we derived and prioritized fruitful and uncovered directions for future research, which build great potential for researchers in this field. Besides that, we derived important implications for managerial action. Therefore, our work contributes to the conceptual research stream by being the first paper, giving a comprehensive and structured overview of the existing research about pricing strategy in retailing and by summarizing and prioritizing relevant findings both for the academic world and for retailing practice.

Second, we are the first to empirically answer the question: how does a hybrid versus a clearly aligned EDLP or Hi-Lo pricing strategy affect retailer performance. Many studies have investigated the factors that affect a retailer's decision to pursue a particular pricing strategy (i.e., antecedents to pricing strategy), however the theoretical and empirical link between store-level pricing strategy and store performance is not investigated to date. For our investigation, we obtained a large-scale dataset from SymphonyIRI, consisting of objective weekly scanner data from 931 retail stores over a two-year period in Germany. Out of this dataset, which was obtained on the very detailed EAN- or product-level, we built a representative product basket with 34 categories. Based on these data and to answer the above mentioned research question, we developed a detailed measurement of our focal construct – the pricing strategy alignment of each store – which was claimed frequently by prior research, we measured and tested for the effects of a retailers' pricing strategy alignment on firm performance, and we identified and examined variables that may moderate the relationship between the pricing strategy alignment and retailer performance: sales dollars per sqm and sales volume per sqm. Thereby, we considered market, store and competitor factors as moderators of this relation. Our results show that there is a nonlinear relationship between pricing strategy alignment and retailers' sales dollars and sales volume per sqm. Quite simply, we show for the first time that grocery retailers should avoid getting stuck in the middle when it comes to pricing strategies. Retailers are better off pursuing either a Hi-Lo or an EDLP pricing strategy in order to achieve the highest sales performance. To not get stuck in the middle with the pricing strategy is even more important for non-discounters and for retail stores, located in areas with higher buying power. Our study extends existing literature as to our knowledge, it is the first study that measured and compared retail pricing strategies at the store-level using objective scanner data. Thus, despite the fact that most retailers are pursuing hybrid pricing strategies, there has not been an empirical or theoretical test to answer how a hybrid pricing strategy impacts store sales performance. Finally, we detect many fruitful areas for future research connected with some limitations of our empirical research. Furthermore, we derived insightful implications for retailing management. In summary, our study contributes to the understanding of retail pricing for both researchers and managers in marketing.

Third, we examined the price promotion activity at the category level and its impact on the retailer performance in terms of productivity of the sales area. This topic is of high relevance especially in the retailing practice, as shown by the fact that in the German grocery retailing sector, the number of price promotions is currently on a new record-high: almost every fifth Euro in grocery retailing is now achieved with products that are particularly advertised or offered at reduced price. Furthermore, in our interviews that we conducted with CEOs and high-ranked managers in the retailing industry, consultants and scientists in our qualitative pre-study, many interviewees stressed the importance of knowing more about the effect of price promotions on the sales dollars of a retailer at the category level. That's why we wanted to shed light on this field of research and conducted our category-level study about price promotion activities. For this study, we used the same data as in our empirical examination in chapter 3, containing objective weekly scanner data collected at the store-level received from 931 different retail stores in Germany, over a two-year period. Our results show different implications regarding the price promotion activity for different categories. Based on our results, we develop five groups of relationships between the price promotion activity in the category and the store performance:

1. no relationship with recommendation "no price promotion activity" for categories chocolate/cereal bars and auto dish

2. a positive linear relationship with recommendation "high price promotion activity" for categories brandy/cognac, heavy duty detergents, shower gel and shampoo,

3. a negative linear relationship with recommendation "low price promotion activity" for categories margarine, cream cheese, chocolate, juices, roasted coffee, yoghurt, pralines, dog food, ham and sausage, soups and stews, salty snacks, air freshener and rice

4. an inverted u-shaped relationship with recommendation "medium price promotion activity" for categories bathroom tissue, soft drinks, total hand & body care, toothpaste, ketchup, spirituous beverages, fruit gums, cereals, liquors, instant/convenient food, sparkling wine/champaign, sweet spread, frozen pizza, deodorants and

5. a u-shaped relationship with recommendation "either high or low price promotion activity" for category general purpose cleaner.

The study contributes to a better understanding of how to handle different categories with regard to the pricing promotion activity with concrete implications for retail managers.

This dissertation builds an extensive contribution to two important research streams: the pricing research and the strategy research. It starts with a comprehensive examination of the highly relevant topic of pricing strategy in retailing with a detailed theoretical foundation and analysis of the topic. Based on that, we conducted an empirical study about the impact of the pricing strategy in retailing at the store level on store performance and its moderating effects, followed by another empirical examination about the price promotion activity at the category level and its impact on store performance. Each study concludes with fruitful implications both for future research and for managerial action.

Appendix

Expert Interview Guidelines

We asked each interviewee a set of nine questions along the following lines:

1. From your perspective, is there anything unique about a pricing strategy for retailers versus a pricing strategy for other organizations, e.g. consumer goods manufacturers?
2. According to you, what are the main pricing strategies in the German retail market?
3. How relevant do you think the topic of Hi-Lo vs. EDLP pricing strategies is?
4. How important are price promotions for retailers and manufacturers? What experiences have you had with using these tactics?
5. Are pricing strategies like Hi-Lo and EDLP determined at the store-level, or at the category-, product or brand-level?
6. To what extent is the pricing strategy determined by the headquarters? How much decision power do single store managers have?
7. What do you think constitutes a Hi-Lo versus an EDLP pricing strategy? What are the components that make up each of the two strategies?
8. What are retailer specific outcomes affected by Hi-Lo / EDLP pricing strategy? What are advantages and disadvantages of each?
9. What are the determinants of a Hi-Lo / EDLP pricing strategy in retailing? What factors moderate the effect of each of those strategies on store performance?

References

Ahlert D, Kenning P (2007) Handelsmarketing. Springer, Heidelberg

Ailawadi KL, Beauchamp JP, Donthu N, Gauri DK, Shankar V (2009) Communication and Promotion Decisions in Retailing: A Review and Directions for Future Research. Journal of Retailing 85(1):42-55

Aldrich H (1976) Resource Dependence and Interorganizational Relations: Local Employment Service Offices and Social Services Sector Organizations. Administration and Society 7(4):419-454

Aldrich H, Pfeffer JS (1976) Environments of Organizations. In: Inkeles A, Coleman J, Smelser N. (eds) Annual Review of Sociology 2:79-105

Allen RS, Helms MM, Takeda MB, White CS (2007) Porter's Generic Strategies: An Exploratory Study of their Use in Japan. Journal of Business Strategies 24(1): 69-90

Anderson C, Zeithaml C (1984) Stage of the Product Life Cycle, Business Strategy and Business Performance. Academy of Management Journal 27(1):1-24

Bailey AA (2008) Evaluating consumer response to EDLPs. Journal of Retailing and Consumer Services 15(3):211-223

Bain JS (1956) Barriers to New Competition: Their Character and Consequences in Manufacturing Industries. Harvard University Press, Cambridge

Barney JB (1991) Firm Resources and Sustained Competitive Advantage. Journal of Management 17(1):99-120

Barth K, Hartmann M, Schröder H (2007) Betriebswirtschaftslehre des Handels. 6. Aufl. Wiesbaden, Gabler

Bell DR, Ho T-H, Tang CS (1998) Determining Where to Shop: Fixed and Variable Costs of Shopping. Journal of Marketing Research 35(3):352-369

Bell DR, Lattin JM (1998) Shopping Behavior and Consumer Preference for Store Price Format: Why "Large Basket" Shoppers Prefer EDLP. Marketing Science 17(1):66-88

Bendapudi N, Leone RP (2002) Managing Business-to-Business Customer Relationships Following Key Contact Employee Turnover in a Vendor Firm. Journal of Marketing 66(2): 83-101

Berekoven L (1995) Erfolgreiches Einzelhandelsmarketing. 2. Aufl. Beck, München

Boatwright P, Dhar S, Rossi PE (2004) The Role of Retail Competition, Demographics and Account Retail Strategy as Drivers of Promotional Sensitivity. Quantitative Marketing and Economics 2(2):169-190

Bolton RN, Shankar V (2003) An empirically derived taxonomy of retailer pricing and promotion strategies. Journal of Retailing 79(4):213-224

Bolton RN, Shankar V, Montoya DY (2010) Recent Trends and Emerging Practices in Retailer Pricing. In: Krafft M, Mantrala MK (eds) Retailing in the 21st Century: Current and Future Trends. 2nd ed. Springer, Berlin, Wiesbaden:301-318

Bolton RN, Shankar V, Montoya DY (2007) Recent Trends and Emerging Practices in Retailer Pricing. In: Krafft M, Mantrala MK (eds) Retailing in the 21st Century: Current and Future Trends. Springer, Berlin, Wiesbaden:255-269

Briesch RA, Chintagunta PK, Fox EJ (2009) How Does Assortment Affect Grocery Store Choice?. Journal of Marketing Research 46(2): 176-189

Brown FE (1969) Price Image Versus Price Reality. Journal of Marketing Research 6(2): 185-191

Cataluna FJR, Franco MJS, Ramos AFV (2005) Are hypermarket prices different from discount store prices? Journal of Product and Brand Management 14(4):330-337

Dhar SK, Hoch SJ (1997) Why Store Brand Penetration Varies by Retailer. Marketing Science 16(3):208-227

Diller H (2008) Preispolitik. 4. Aufl. Kohlhammer, Stuttgart

Dutta S, Zbaracki MJ, Bergen M (2003) Pricing Process as a Capability: A Resource-Based Perspective. Strategic Management Journal 24(7):615-630

El Husseini S, Fassnacht M (2012) Price Promotion Activity at the Category Level: Less is More? Unpublished manuscript

Ellickson PB, Misra S (2008) Supermarket Pricing Strategies. Marketing Science 27(5):811-828

Fassnacht M, El Husseini S (2012) EDLP versus Hi-Lo Pricing Strategies in Retailing - A State of the Art Article. Zeitschrift für Betriebswirtschaft, forthcoming

Fassnacht M, El Husseini S, DeKinder JS (2012) Don't Get Stuck in the Middle! A Comparison of Pure versus Hybrid Pricing Strategies in Retailing. Unpublished manuscript

Gauri D, Janakiraman R, Kalayanam K, Kannan PK, Ratchford B, Song R, Tolerico S (2010) Strategic Online and Offline Retail Pricing: A Review and Research Agenda. Journal of Interactive Marketing 24(2):138-154

Gauri DK, Trivedi M, Grewal D (2008) Understanding the Determinants of Retail Strategy: An Empirical Analysis. Journal of Retailing 84(3):256-267

Gedenk K (2002) Verkaufsförderung. Vahlen, München

Ginsberg A, Venkatraman N (1985) Contingency Perspectives of Organizational Strategy: A Critical Review of the Empirical Research. Academy of Management Review 10 (3):421-434

Grewal D, Janakiraman R, Kalayanam K, Kannan PK, Ratchford B, Song R, Tolerico S (2010) Strategic Online and Offline Retail Pricing: A Review and Research Agenda. Journal of Interactive Marketing 24(2): 138-154

Grewal D, Levy M (2007) Retailing Research: Past, present, and future. Journal of Retailing 83(4):447-464

Hambrick DC (1983a) An Empirical Typology of Mature Industrial-Product Environments. Academy of Management Journal 26(2):213-230

Hambrick DC (1983b) High Profit Strategies in Mature Capital Goods Industries: A Contingency Approach. Academy of Management Journal 26 (4):687-707

Hill CWL (1988) Differentiation Versus Low Cost or Differentiation and Low Cost: A Contingency Framework. Academy of Management Review 13(3): 401-412.

Ho H, Wang FY (2011) Prestige, Parallel or Predatory – Pricing Strategies amongst Taiwanese Universities. International Journal of Marketing Studies 3(3): 67-77

Hoch SJ, Drèze X, Purk ME (1994) EDLP, Hi-Lo, and Margin Arithmetic. Journal of Marketing 58(4):16-27

Holton RH (1957) Price Discrimination at Retail: The Supermarket Case. The Journal of Industrial Economics 6(1):13-32

Ingene CA, Brown JR (1987) The Structure of Gasoline Retailing. Journal of Retailing 63(4): 365-392

Kieser A (2006) Der Situative Ansatz. In: Kieser A (Hrsg) Organisationstheorien. 6. Aufl. Kohlhammer, Stuttgart:215-239

Kim E, Nam D, Stimpert JL (2004) Testing the Applicability of Porter's Generic Strategies in the Digital Age: A Study of Korean Cyber Malls. Journal of Business Strategies 21(1): 19-45

Kocas C, Bohlmann JD (2008) Segmented Switchers and Retailer Pricing Strategies. Journal of Marketing 72(3):124-142

Kohli AK, Jaworski BJ (1990) Market Orientation: The Construct, Research Propositions, and Managerial Implications. Journal of Marketing 54(2): 1-18

Kopalle P, Biswas D, Chintagunta PK, Fan J, Pauwels K, Ratchford BT, Sills JA (2009) Retailer Pricing and Competitive Effects. Journal of Retailing 85(1):56-70

Lal R, Rao R (1997) Supermarket Competition: The Case of Every Day Low Pricing. Marketing Science 16(1):60-80

Lattin JM, Ortmeyer G (1991) A Theoretical Rationale for Everyday Low Pricing by Grocery Retailers. Research Paper 1144, Stanford University

Levy M, Grewal D, Kopalle PK, Hess JD (2004) Emerging trends in retail pricing practice: implications for research. Journal of Retailing 80(3):13-21

Levy M. Weitz BA (2007) Retailing Management. McGraw Hill, New York

Liebmann H-P, Zentes J, Swoboda B (2008) Handelsmanagement. 2. Aufl. Vahlen, München

Mason ES (1957) Economic Concentration and the Monopoly Problem. Harvard University Press, Cambridge

Menon A, Bharadwaj SG, Adidam PT, Edison SW (1999) Antecedents and Consequences of Marketing Strategy Making: A Model and a Test. Journal of Marketing 63(2): 18-40

Miller D, Friesen PH (1986) Porter's (1980) Generic Strategies and Performance: An Empirical Examination with American Data. Organization Studies 7(3): 255-261

Möhlenbruch D, von Wichert G (2002) Die Bedeutung des Ressourcenorientierten Ansatzes für die Strategieentwicklung im Einzelhandel. In: Trommsdorff V (Hrsg) Handelsforschung 2001/02. BBE-Verlag, Köln: 53-72

Monroe KB (2003) Pricing: making profitable decisions. 3rd ed. McGraw-Hill, New York

Montgomery AL (1997) Creating Micro-Marketing Pricing Strategies Using Supermarket Scanner Data. Marketing Science 16(4):315-337

Murray AI (1988) A Contingency View of Porter's "Generic Strategies". Academy of Management Review 13(3): 390-400

Müller-Hagedorn L, Natter M (2011) Handelsmarketing. 5. Aufl. Kohlhammer, Stuttgart

Müller-Hagedorn L, Preißner M (2006) Zur Beurteilung von Dauertiefpreisen und Aktionspreisen aus Konsumentensicht. Handel im Fokus 58(1):5-20

Müller-Stewens G, Lechner C (2003) Strategisches Management. 2. Aufl. Schäffer-Poeschel, Stuttgart

Mulhern FJ, Leone RP (1990) Retail Promotional Advertising. Journal of Business Research 21(3):179-194

Nagle TT, Hogan JE, Zale J (2011) The Strategy and Tactics of Pricing. 5th ed. Pearson, New Jersey

Neslin SA, Shoemaker RW (1994) The Relationship between Retail EDLP Pricing and Repeat Purchasing. Working paper.

Nijs VR, Srinivasan S, Pauwels K (2007) Retail-Price Drivers and Retailer Profits. Marketing Science 26(4):473-487

Nyström H, Tamsons H, Thams R (1975) An Experiment in Price Generalization and Discrimination. Journal of Marketing Research 12(2):177-181

Ortmeyer G, Quelch JA, Salmon W (1991) Restoring Credibility to Retail Pricing. Sloan Management Review 33(1):55-66

Pechtl H (2004) Profiling intrinsic deal proneness for HILO and EDLP price promotion strategies. Journal of Retailing and Consumer Services 11(4):223-233

Pechtl H (2005) Preispolitik. Lucius & Lucius, Stuttgart

Pertusa-Ortega EM, Molina-Azoin JF, Claver-Cortez E (2009) Competitive Strategies and Firm Performance: A Comparative Analysis of Pure, Hybrid and 'Stuck-in-the-middle' Strategies in Spanish Firms. British Journal of Management 20(4): 508-523.

Pervaiz KA, and Rafiq M (1992) Implanting Competitive Strategy: a Contingency Approach. Journal of Marketing Management 8(1): 49-67

Pfeffer JS (1972) Merger as a Response to Organizational Interdependence. Administrative Science Quarterly 17(3):382-391

Pfeffer JS (1978) Organizational Design. AHM Pub. Co., Arlington Heights

Pfeffer JS, Salancik GR (1978) The External Control of Organizations: A Resource Dependence Perspective. Harper and Row, New York

Popkowski Leszczyc PTL, Sinha A, Sahgal A (2004) The effect of multi-purpose shopping on pricing and location strategy for grocery stores. Journal of Retailing 80(2):85-99

Popkowski Leszczyc PTL, Sinha A, Timmermans HJP (2000) Consumer Store Choice Dynamics: An Analysis of the Competitive Market Structure for Grocery Stores. Journal of Retailing 73(3):323-345

Porter ME (1991) Towards a Dynamic Theory of Strategy. Strategic Management Journal 12(8):95-117

Porter ME (1980) Competitive Strategy: Techniques for Analyzing Industries and Competitors. The Free Press, New York

Proff H (2002) Konsistente Gesamtunternehmensstrategien. Wiesbaden, Deutscher Universitäts-Verlag

Rao, AR. (2005) The Quality of Price as a Quality Cue. Journal of Marketing Research 42(4): 401-405

Rao VR (1984) Pricing Research in Marketing: The State of the Art. Journal of Business 57(1):39-60

Rao VR, Kartono B (2009) Pricing objectives and strategies: a cross-country survey. In: Rao VR (ed.) Handbook of Pricing Research in Marketing. Elgar, Cheltenham:9-36

Routroy S, Singh D (2011) Development of Optimal Pricing Strategy for Perishable Products. The IUP Journal of Supply Chain Management 8(1): 37-44

Rudolph T, Wagner T (2003) Preis-Image Politik im Handel. In: Diller H, Herrmann A (Hrsg) Handbuch Preispolitk. Gabler, Wiesbaden:177-198

Scheuch F (2007) Marketing. 6. Aufl. Vahlen, München

Schuppar B (2006) Preismanagement: Konzeption, Umsetzung und Erfolgsauswirkungen im Business-to-Business-Bereich. Gabler, Wiesbaden.

Sebastian K-H, Maessen A (2003) Optionen im strategischen Preismanagement. In: Diller H, Herrmann A (Hrsg) Handbuch Preispolitk. Gabler, Wiesbaden:51-68

Shah A (2007) Strategic Groups in Retailing Based on Porter's Generic Market Based Strategies. Marketing Management Journal 17(1): 151-170

Shankar V, Bolton RN (2004) An Empirical Analysis of Determinants of Retailer Pricing Strategy. Journal of Retailing 23(1):28-49. In: Diller H, Herrmann A (Hrsg) Handbuch Preispolitik

Shankar V, Krishnamurthi L (1996) Relating Price Sensitivity to Retailer Promotional Variables and Pricing Policy: An Empirical Analysis. Journal of Retailing 72(3):249-272

Shiv B, Carmon Z, Ariely D (2005) Placebo Effects of Marketing Actions: Consumers May Get What They Pay For. Journal of Marketing Research 42(4): 383-393

Simon H (2004) Ertragssteigerung durch effektivere Pricing-Prozesse. Zeitschrift für Betriebswirtschaft 74(11):1083-1102

Simon H, Fassnacht M (2009) Preismanagement, 3. Aufl. Gabler, Wiesbaden

Suri R, Manchanda RV, Kohli CS (2000) Brand evaluations: a comparison of fixed price and discounted price offers. Journal of Product and Brand Management 9(3):193-206

Suri R, Manchanda RV, Kohli CS (2002) Comparing fixed price and discounted price strategies: the role of affect on evaluations. Journal of Product and Brand Management 11(3):160-173

Tang CS, Bell DR, Ho T-H (2001) Store Choice and Shopping Behavior: How Price Format Works. California Management Review 43(2):56-74

Tellis GJ (1986) Beyond the Many Faces of Price: An Integration of Pricing Strategies. Journal of Marketing 50(4):146-160

Thornhill S, White RE (2007) Strategic Purity: A Multi-Industry Evaluation of Pure vs. Hybrid Business Strategies. Strategic Management Journal 28(5): 553-561

Tsiros M, Hardesy DM (2010) Ending a Price Promotion: Retracting It in One Step Or Phasing It Out Gradually. Journal of Marketing 74(1):49-64

Tuli KR, Kohli AK, Bharadwaj SG (2007) Rethinking Customer Solutions: From Product Bundles to Relational Processes. Journal of Marketing 71(3): 1-17

Van Heerde HJ, Gijsbrechts E, Pauwels K (2008) Winners and Losers in a Major Price War. Journal of Marketing Research 45 (5): 499-518

Van Ittersum K, Joost MEP, Wansink B (2010) Trying Harder and Doing Worse: How Grocery Shoppers Track In-Store Spendings,. Journal of Marketing 74(2): 90-104

Voss GB, Seiders K (2003) Exploring the effect of retail sector and firm characteristics on retail price promotion strategy. Journal of Retailing 79(1):37-52

Wernerfelt B (1984) A Resource-Based View of the Firm. Strategic Management Journal 5(2):4-12

Wiltinger K (1998) Preismanagement in der unternehmerischen Praxis: Probleme der organisatorischen Implementierung. Gabler, Wiesbaden

Wright P, Kroll M, Kedia B, Pringle C (1990) Strategic Profiles, Market Share, and Business Performance. Industrial Management 32(3): 23-28

Zeithaml VA, Varadarajan PR, Zeithaml CP (1988) The Contingency Approach: Its Foundations and Relevance to Theory Building and Research in Marketing. European Journal of Marketing 22(7):37-64

Schriften zu Marketing und Handel

Herausgegeben von Martin Fassnacht

www.peterlang.com